THE BEGINNERS GUIDE TO

THE WONDERFUL WORLD OF WINE

To Jeff — Thanks for the interview

Bob Dunlap

Printed in Victoria, Canada

National Library of Canada Cataloguing in Publication Data

A cataloguing record for this book that includes the U.S. Library of Congress Classification number, the Library of Congress Call number and the Dewey Decimal cataloguing code is available from the National Library of Canada. The complete cataloguing record can be obtained from the National Library's online database at: www.nlc-bnc.ca/amicus/index-e.html

ISBN: 1-4120-1889-7

TRAFFORD

This book was published *on-demand* in cooperation with Trafford Publishing.
On-demand publishing is a unique process and service of making a book available for retail sale to the public taking advantage of on-demand manufacturing and Internet marketing. **On-demand publishing** includes promotions, retail sales, manufacturing, order fulfilment, accounting and collecting royalties on behalf of the author.

Suite 6E, 2333 Government St., Victoria, B.C. V8T 4P4, CANADA

Phone	250-383-6864	Toll-free	1-888-232-4444 (Canada & US)
Fax	250-383-6804	E-mail	sales@trafford.com
Web site www.trafford.com		TRAFFORD PUBLISHING IS A DIVISION OF TRAFFORD HOLDINGS LTD.	
Trafford Catalogue #03-2267		www.trafford.com/robots/03-2267.html	

10   9   8   7   6   5   4   3   2

Dedicated to my offspring

Sher, Dawn, Richard

Todd and Kelly

In memory of:

TONY LUCIANO (TUPPER)

JIM BRADY

Acknowledgements:

I shall be forever grateful to my loving daughter Dawn, whose devotion, fortitude and perseverance led to the completion of this book.

Without her encouragement and support, it simply could not have happened.

Special thanks to :

Sher Grelick, Dawn Marlowe, Adola DeWolf, Todd Quinlan, Don Taylor, Mike O'Hare, Mike Bennett, Jim Brady, Don Hendricks, Vin Lombard and Phil Adams, for their contributions to this book.

During my forty years working in the wine business, I accumulated much in the way of useful information as well as trivia about wines that I am sure any neophyte or wine lover will enjoy reading.

While you may not become a connoisseur, you will increase your knowledge about "wines of the world".

" Salute"

Bob Quinlan

Certificates:

Honorary Member-
The Spanish Wine Society For Promoting Fine Spanish Wines
Director-Angel Santiago

Macon En France
Robert T. Quinlan, Honorary Ambassadeur Exttraordinaire.
Le President Director General- Charles Piat

Certificate of Merit For Understanding Romanian Wines
General Director Vine*Port Gr.Stancivlesca

Weingut Hierstein Am Rheim
Meritous Service Award For The Promotion of Fine German Wines
Georg Karl Ludwig Schmitt Director General

Robert T. Quinlan, Selected as Local Agent For the Promotion of the Fine Wines of France.
Roland Thevenin
MAYOR OF SAINT ROMAIN

ABOUT THE AUTHOR

The author is a decorated veteran of World War II having served with the
5TH Air Force, 3rd Bomb Group, 13th Squadron in the Pacific area joining his group in
Australia in 1942, then through New Guinea, many islands in the Philippines, Okinawa,
and finally landing in Japan with the first Americans to occupy Japan, four days before
the surrender signing on September 2, 1945, returning to be discharged from the
Air Corps on December 23, 1945.

Robert Quinlan began his career in the wines in the early 1950's while accepting a
position with Ernest & Julio Wine Company of Modesto, California.
It was here that Bob had the opportunity to walk the vast vineyards by day, absorbing
row after row of fragrant ripening grapes, while nightfall offered an exploration of
extensive cellars containing vats of aging wine waiting to be bottled.

As the fragrant grapes had permeated Bob's senses on that first vineyard walk, it was the
beginning of his long love affair with wine. Reading and studying everything possible
about wines, Bob traveled to vineyards in France, Germany, Romania, Italy and other
areas throughout the world where he was fortunate to have sampled some of the finest
wines available. Bob's quest for knowledge and his desire to impassion others, led him to
pioneer wine tastings in his hometown of Rochester, New York. Backed by local liquor
stores, weekly regional wine tastings became newsworthy as the place to be… and be
seen.

After nine years with the Gallo, Bob was approached by Monsieur Henry Imported Wine
Company, then independently owned by the Feinberg family, to take a position as State
Manager. This served to further his commitment and passion in the knowledge of wines
earning him the respect of his fellow aficionados and connoisseurs.

In 1972 when Monsieur Henry became a Division of Pepsico Company, Bob was
promoted to the position of Division Manager where he held the position until his
retirement in 1986.

Reevaluating the allure of his retirement, Bob soon found himself accepting numerous
speaking engagements and seminars, finding much joy in sharing his vast knowledge
with impassioned like minded people.

To this day he can be found heading up a wine tasting be it local or abroad…a
"California Cabernet or a Chateau Mouton Rothschild 1945 it matters not, for there ia a
wine to suit every discriminating taste".

INTRODUCTION

There are many tales and legends about wine that go back before the time of Christ. The history of wine is deeply rooted in traditions, customs and the souls of people. Alberto Savinio once stated, "Tell us your history through your wine."

Twelve centuries ago, Charlemagne stood where the Rhine turns west, glanced across the snowy slopes that glistened in the spring sunlight, sighted one patch that was bare and said, "Secure the heights and set a vineyard where the ground is clear," and it was done.

The castle of Johannisberg was built above the vineyard, and ever since, Schloss Johannnisberg wines have carried the legend around the world.

While the legend of Johannisberg is just one of the many stories compiled in this book, there are many such tales, some are true, some are fascinating and some are hard to believe.

So with this in mind, this book was published to add a little more enjoyment and perhaps bring a smile to one's face as they sip a wine with a legend or tale related to its tradition and winemaking history.

Robert T. Quinlan

PART ONE

Table of Contents:

I.   Learn by Tasting

II.   Wine Faults

III. Some Key Words to Describe Wine

IV.   Serving Wine

V.   Wine and Food

VI.   Ordering in Restaurants

I.   Learn by Tasting

1. **Look at the Wine:**
Is it clear and brilliant? Is it light, medium or dark? Color tells age. An off color suggests an off wine.

2. **Smell the Wine:**
More of the wine's taste is odor. Note the odor of the grape. The Melon de Bourguignon aroma of a Muscadet, the fresh fruit of Beaujolais, the black currant, truffle odor of Claret. Swirl the glass to release more aroma and bouquet. The locked up complex flavors in an especially mature red wine, the perfume expands as the wine aerates in the glass.

3. **Sip the wine:**
Don't swallow yet; let it roll in your mouth because most of your taste buds are situated on the sides and back of the tongue. Is the wine light, medium or full in body (the weight of the wine)? Is it dry, sweet, acid, or astringent (too much Tannin)? Is it too alcoholic, or is it well balanced with sugar, acids, extracts, etc., all in proper proportion? Very good wines have a long, lingering finish.

4. **Tasting is the Key to Wine Knowledge:**
It is fun to talk about wine, but learning the techniques of tasting will increase your knowledge and enjoyment of it. The visual, olfactory and gustatory senses all play a part in wine tasting.

II.   Wine Faults

Wine is a living thing that is subject to disease and other ailments despite the strict hygienic controls in the modern bottling. Learning to detect faults is another key to wine knowledge.

1.   **Corked Wine:**
       Symptoms: the cork smells unpleasant, the wine tastes of fungus.
       Cause of fungus: A spoiled cork.

2.   **Cloudiness:**
       Symptoms, a cloudy haze in the wine that does not settle.
       Causes: Excess protein, metal contamination or bacterial action.

3.   **Second Fermentation:**
       Symptoms, bubbles, cloudiness, a nasty smell and taste.
       Cause: The yeast that is still present ferments.

4.   **Crystalline Deposits:**
       Symptoms: delicate flakes that settle when the bottle is standing.
       Cause: low temperatures precipitate excess tartrates. The tartrates are harmless and don't hurt the wine.

5.   **Oxidation:**
       Symptoms: an unpleasant smell, a darkening of the color, the wine ranges from bit off to undrinkable.
       Cause: exposure to air, either before or after bottling.

6.   **Excessive Sulfur:**
       Symptoms: a pungent smell of sulfur. Let the bottle stand to allow the smell to fade.

III. Some Key Words to Describe Wines

1. **Acetic:**   Sour, vinegary odor, also called volatile acidity.

2. **Acid:**   A sharp, tart effect of the green fruit of young wine, which is desirable for a wine that mellows with age.

3. **Aroma:**   The perfume of fresh fruit. The bouquet with age replaces it.

4. **Astringent:**   A rough, puckery taste caused by tannin. It diminishes with age.

5. **Big:**   Full of body and flavor.

6. **Clean:**   Well constituted without smells or offensive taste.

7. **Closed:**   Shows no character yet, especially in young reds.

8. **Cloying:**   Too sweet with too little acidity.

9. **Earthy:**   Gout de terrior, or the taste of soil.

10. **Fat:**   Full bodied but flabby for whites, soft and mature for reds.

11. **Flabby:**   Too soft, almost limp.

12.	**Hard:**	Tannic, without charm or softness.
13.	**Long:**	The flavor lingers in the mouth, opposite of short.
14.	**Musty:**	Moldy, bad odor and stale flavor.
15.	**Nose:**	Encompasses aroma and bouquet.
16.	**Petillant:**	Effervescent with light sparkle.
17.	**Piquant:**	Dry and crisply acid.
18.	**Rounded:**	Well balanced and complete.
19.	**Sharp:**	Excessive acidity
20.	**Thin:**	Lacking body and alcohol, too watery to be called light.
21.	**Woody:**	Oak odors and flavors from storage in casks too long.
22.	**Self-Descriptive Words:**	Bitter, clear, cloudy, course, dry, elegant, finesse, flat, flowery, full, harsh, insipid, lively, luscious, mellow, noble, smooth, soft, spicy, sweet, tart, tannic, vigorous, watery

IV. Serving Wine

- Serve reds at room temperature.

- Slightly chill (one hour in the refrigerator) whites, rosès, sparkling and some light reds (like Beaujolais).

- Serve dry before sweet, white before red and young wines before old ones.

- Glasses should be clear and stemmed (to hold so it will not be warmed by your hand).

- The flute shaped is best for champagne (the bubbles last longer).

- Fill the glass half full (in order to swirl the wine). You decant to separate a red wine from its sediment (most wines have no sediment) and to let them "breathe" or receive oxygen to release the bouquet.

V.   Wine and Foods

Enjoy exploring different "marriages" of wine and food, but also be aware there are time-tested guidelines to follow, such as:

1.	**Hors d'oeuvre:**	Serve light dry white or rosè wine.
2.	**Fish:**	Serve dry or sweet white wine or rosè.
3.	**White Meat and Poultry:**	Dry white or light red wine.
4.	**Red Meat:**	Full bodied red wine.
5.	**Cheese:**	Generally all wines can be served but red wines are best with pungent cheeses and white with mild cheese, such as goat cheese.
6.	**Dessert and Fruit:**	Sweet white or champagne.
7.	**Chinese Food:**	Medium dry or medium sweet white wines.

8.   Sparkling wines and Rosè complement many kinds of foods. However, wine does not go well with some foods, such as: those heavily flavored with vinegar, citrus juices or curry powder (Indian food), Russian shcki or borscht and Hungarian stuffed cabbage.

9.   Wines and food balance each other, enhancing each other's flavors. Wines should stand up to, but not overwhelm the food. Serve light wines with delicate foods, more full bodied with heavier foods.

VI.   Ordering in Restaurants

When faced with a wine list, you want to take command and order good selections confidently. Many restaurants overprice wines, but they should compensate by having a compendate sommelier (a wine butler). Use him to good effect by asking questions.

The house wine should be very sound. If you ask if its dry and he says medium dry, that usually means it's medium sweet. If you order fish, a Loire, regional Bordeaux, or Chenin Blanc are good, inexpensive selections. For your meat courses, an Italian, California, New York State, Spanish, or Rhone can be fine choices since Bordeaux and estate bottled Burgundies are often very high priced. A good server can usually recommend a good wine. Ask his or her suggestions.

When served, smell the cork for bad odors, taste the wine for oxidation and check clearness etc. (refer to the wine faults page). Send a wine back only if it is faulty, not if you don't like it. If you don't know vintages, again ask the server. Usually the price reflects good and bad vintages. If the server sees you are a wine enthusiast, he will recommend good wines from the wine list.

I.   Learn by Tasting

II.   Wine Faults

III. Some Key Words to Describe Wine

IV.   Serving Wine

V.   Wine and Food

VI.   Ordering in Restaurants

I.   Learn by Tasting

1.   Look at the Wine:
Is it clear and brilliant? Is it light, medium or dark? Color tells age. An off color suggests an off wine.

2.   Smell the Wine:
More of the wine's taste is odor. Note the odor of the grape. The Melon de Bourguignon aroma of a Muscadet, the fresh fruit of Beaujolais, the black currant, truffle odor of Claret. Swirl the glass to release more aroma and bouquet. The locked up complex flavors in an especially mature red wine, the perfume expands as the wine aerates in the glass.

3.   Sip the wine:
Don't swallow yet; let it roll in your mouth because most of your taste buds are situated on the sides and back of the tongue. Is the wine light, medium or full in body (the weight of the wine)? Is it dry, sweet, acid, or astringent (too much Tannin)? Is it too alcoholic, or is it well balanced with sugar, acids, extracts, etc., all in proper proportion? Very good wines have a long, lingering finish.

4.   Tasting is the Key to Wine Knowledge:
It is fun to talk about wine, but learning the techniques of tasting will increase your knowledge and enjoyment of it. The visual, olfactory and gustatory senses all play a part in wine tasting.

II.   Wine Faults

Wine is a living thing that is subject to disease and other ailments despite the strict hygienic controls in the modern bottling. Learning to detect faults is another key to wine knowledge.

1.   Corked Wine:
Symptoms: the cork smells unpleasant, the wine tastes of fungus.
Cause of fungus: A spoiled cork.

2.   Cloudiness:
Symptoms, a cloudy haze in the wine that does not settle.
Causes: Excess protein, metal contamination or bacterial action.

3.   Second Fermentation:
Symptoms, bubbles, cloudiness, a nasty smell and taste.
Cause: The yeast that is still present ferments.

4.   Crystalline Deposits:
Symptoms: delicate flakes that settle when the bottle is standing.
Cause: low temperatures precipitate excess tartrates. The tartrates are harmless and don't hurt the wine.

5.   Oxidation:
Symptoms: an unpleasant smell, a darkening of the color, the wine ranges from bit off to undrinkable.
Cause: exposure to air, either before or after bottling.

6.   Excessive Sulfur:
Symptoms: a pungent smell of sulfur. Let the bottle stand to allow the smell to fade.

III. Some Key Words to Describe Wines

1.	**Acetic:**	Sour, vinegary odor, also called volatile acidity.
2.	**Acid:**	A sharp, tart effect of the green fruit of young wine, which is desirable for a wine that mellows with age.
3.	**Aroma:**	The perfume of fresh fruit. The bouquet with age replaces it.
4.	**Astringent:**	A rough, puckery taste caused by tannin. It diminishes with age.
5.	**Big:**	Full of body and flavor.
6.	**Clean:**	Well constituted without smells or offensive taste.
7.	**Closed:**	Shows no character yet, especially in young reds.
8.	**Cloying:**	Too sweet with too little acidity.
9.	**Earthy:**	Gout de terrior, or the taste of soil.
10.	**Fat:**	Full bodied but flabby for whites, soft and mature for reds.
11.	**Flabby:**	Too soft, almost limp.

12.	**Hard:**	Tannic, without charm or softness.
13.	**Long:**	The flavor lingers in the mouth, opposite of short.
14.	**Musty:**	Moldy, bad odor and stale flavor.
15.	**Nose:**	Encompasses aroma and bouquet.
16.	**Petillant:**	Effervescent with light sparkle.
17.	**Piquant:**	Dry and crisply acid.
18.	**Rounded:**	Well balanced and complete.
19.	**Sharp:**	Excessive acidity
20.	**Thin:**	Lacking body and alcohol, too watery to be called light.
21.	**Woody:**	Oak odors and flavors from storage in casks too long.
22.	**Self-Descriptive Words:**	Bitter, clear, cloudy, course, dry, elegant, finesse, flat, flowery, full, harsh, insipid, lively, luscious, mellow, noble, smooth, soft, spicy, sweet, tart, tannic, vigorous, watery

IV. Serving Wine

    Serve reds at room temperature.

    Slightly chill (one hour in the refrigerator) whites, rosès, sparkling and some light reds (like Beaujolais).

    Serve dry before sweet, white before red and young wines before old ones.

    Glasses should be clear and stemmed (to hold so it will not be warmed by your hand).

    The flute shaped is best for champagne (the bubbles last longer).

    Fill the glass half full (in order to swirl the wine). You decant to separate a red wine from its sediment (most wines have no sediment) and to let them "breathe" or receive oxygen to release the bouquet.

V.   Wine and Foods

Enjoy exploring different "marriages" of wine and food, but also be aware there are time-tested guidelines to follow, such as:

1.	**Hors d'oeuvre:**	Serve light dry white or rosè wine.
2.	**Fish:**	Serve dry or sweet white wine or rosè.
3.	**White Meat and Poultry:**	Dry white or light red wine.
4.	**Red Meat:**	Full bodied red wine.
5.	**Cheese:**	Generally all wines can be served but red wines are best with pungent cheeses and white with mild cheese, such as goat cheese.
6.	**Dessert and Fruit:**	Sweet white or champagne.
7.	**Chinese Food:**	Medium dry or medium sweet white wines.

8.   Sparkling wines and Rosè complement many kinds of foods. However, wine does not go well with some foods, such as: those heavily flavored with vinegar, citrus juices or curry powder (Indian food), Russian shcki or borscht and Hungarian stuffed cabbage.

9.   Wines and food balance each other, enhancing each other's flavors. Wines should stand up to, but not overwhelm the food. Serve light wines with delicate foods, more full bodied with heavier foods.

VI. Ordering in Restaurants

When faced with a wine list, you want to take command and order good selections confidently. Many restaurants overprice wines, but they should compensate by having a compendate sommelier (a wine butler). Use him to good effect by asking questions.

The house wine should be very sound. If you ask if its dry and he says medium dry, that usually means it's medium sweet. If you order fish, a Loire, regional Bordeaux, or Chenin Blanc are good, inexpensive selections. For your meat courses, an Italian, California, New York State, Spanish, or Rhone can be fine choices since Bordeaux and estate bottled Burgundies are often very high priced. A good server can usually recommend a good wine. Ask his or her suggestions.

When served, smell the cork for bad odors, taste the wine for oxidation and check clearness etc. (refer to the wine faults page). Send a wine back only if it is faulty, not if you don't like it. If you don't know vintages, again ask the server. Usually the price reflects good and bad vintages. If the server sees you are a wine enthusiast, he will recommend good wines from the wine list.

HORSES AND POUILLY FUISSÈ

In the Southern part of the Macon region, near the towns of Pouilly and Fuissè is a huge prow-shaped cliff that was used by the ancient inhabitants as an effective slaughterhouse. Wild horses were trapped and run off the edge of the cliff. The middle class French had a liking for filet de cheval (filet of horse) and this practice was carried on for many years. Some winemakers feel that the build up of bone for hundreds of years provided the calcium that imparts the distinctive taste of Pouilly- Fuissè.

"How goes the time?" 'Tis five o'clock, go fetch a pint of port."

– Author Unknown –

We Palatinates are, I think
A strange race of curious humour;
When we're merry – then we drink!
When we're sad – then we drink more!

– Author Unknown –

"Give me a bowl of wine;
In this I bury all unkindness."

– Julius Caesar –

1

THE HISTORY OF TOASTING

"Let's Drink a Toast" originated back in the early 1600s when some really bad wines were made. Most restaurants and bistros would place a piece of toast atop the wine to mask the offensive taste. After a period of time, people discovered that the toast tasted better than the wine and would pass on the word "drink the toast", instead of the wine, to the friends if they were to visit a certain café with terrible wine.

In the 16th century, the people of France practiced a custom of putting a piece of toast at the bottom of a glass and this was called a "tostee".

The glass was passed from person to person until it reached the one they were honoring and to whose health it was being drunk. This person then ate the "tostee".

The clinking of glasses evolved from an ancient legend that the devil would enter the body with the beverage being consumed, so they created a noise to scare away the evil spirits before they drank a "toast".

Skoal! was handed down to us by the Norsemen who would drink a toast of victory from the "skulls" of their enemies.

Egyptian warriors drank to the health of each other before entering into battle centuries before Christ.

Smashing the wine glasses after drinking a "toast" was considered a great compliment to the one who was being toasted, for it insured that no one could demean the toast thereafter.

Many rituals of drinking a "toast" had developed over the years. In England, a "toast was drunk on bended knees and in Scotland, a "toast" was offered with one foot on the table and the other on the chair with the officers pointing their swords toward heaven. This was a practice of some of England's select societies of officers strictly for the male gender, until a woman was given an honorary membership to one of the exclusive military clubs. This proved to be very interesting to observe – a woman with one leg on the table and one leg on a chair pointing her sword skyward while the officers gazed on with delight.

In Bath, England a different type of "toast" took place in 1653. Two young officers of his majesty's service observed the town's outstanding beauty cross the street to the public bathhouse completely nude. So alluring was her shape and beauty, that one of the officers was about to jump into the bath with Mistress Anne Gaule when he was persuaded by his companion that this would not be fitting and proper for one of his majesty's officers and that the proper thing to do was to fill their wine cups with water from Mistress Ann's bath, and offer a "toast" to her beauty. One officer "threw up" while the other remarked, "I didn't much care for the taste but the 'toast' was befitting to such beauty.

One unique ceremony was conducted in England whereby the "Toaster" would ladle out the wine from the slipper of a beautiful lady.

Gallant Romans would prove their affection by drinking a glass of wine for each letter of his sweetheart's name.

ça

ALCOHOL, A COSMETIC

Even though the Arabs were forbidden to drink alcohol, they did use it in other forms. When an Arab woman would dress up and make herself beautiful for her sheik, the cosmetics used were made by dissolving a powder called kuhl in a fluid from distilled wine. Westerners borrowed the name primarily for the distilled spirit of the wine, thus our work for alcohol.

ça

THE WORLD'S FIRST HANGOVER

Many historians disagree on the exact time and place where the grape was first discovered as an alcoholic beverage. Many claim it was first discovered in China, 2000 years before Christ where it was grown as a food product. One tale relates that one of the vineyard workers left his rice bowl under the vine and as the grapes matured and became overripe, the skin burst and the juices ran down on the other grape skins picking the wild yeast which adheres to the waxy coating and filled the workers rice bowl. With the heat of the sun during daylight hours, the juices fermented. When the worker finally discovered where he had left his bowl, he noticed the refreshing looking juices and drank the new beverage, which gave him a euphoric feeling. Thus it was established that he was the first person on earth to become intoxicated and also the first to experience man's first hangover.

ॐ

"When men drink wine they are rich, they are bush, they push lawsuits, they are happy, they help their friends"

–Aristophanes: "The Knights", 424 B.C. –

ॐ

"The best wine...goeth down sweetly, causing the lips of those that are asleep to speak."

– Solomon's Song 7:9 –

ॐ

THE MYSTERY OF FERMENTATION

There are many unexplainable events that occur during the fermentation process of converting the grapes' sugar into ethyl alcohol. One unique event that has no technical explanation is the restarting of the fermentation that has been stopped by a sudden drop in temperatures. One event heard of in the Bordeaux region is that in a particular chateaux ten vats suddenly stopped fermenting when a cold snap developed on a chilly night. The excited winemaker became panicky and alarmed when he discovered this fatal situation. However, a local technical advisor was consulted and when the technician discovered that the cellar had no heating system of any type, he instructed the cellar master to scour up a wood stove of some sort and place it next to the vat that was in the center of the ten vats that were all in a line; and keep a fire going in the stove to heat the vat it was near. The old cellar master complained that would only heat one vat and his cellar was so large and cold it would be impossible to heat the entire cellar and the remaining nine vats for he could only secure one stove. Have no concern for the other nine vats, the technician replied, if you develop enough heat next to the one vat to get the fermentation started, the other nine will start automatically. To the old winemaker's amazement, when the one vat next to the stove started to ferment, it wasn't long before he could hear the buzzing fermentation activity of the remaining vats. When asked how this was possible, the technician said he had no scientific explanation but just knew it would work.

4

4% PER DAY

In making wine, the rate of alcohol during fermentation is approximately 4% per day, thus a wine that is 14% alcohol by volume would take about 3 ½ days to ferment.

WILD YEAST

The white waxy coat that covers each and every grape is called bloom that contains wild natural yeast. The yeast spores hibernate in the ground during the winter months and, as spring and warm weather develop, they mature and become air-borne and attach themselves to the waxy coating of the grapes. There are many different types of yeast that have been developed by the long process of evolution. Specific strains have developed in each region of Europe that is compatible to the particular grape grown in that region. Example: Montrachet yeast used by many wine makers in the New World is from the Montrachet region in the Cotê de Nuits of France; Champagne yeast is from the Champagne district, etc. etc.

THE FIRST APPELLATION CONTROLEE OF FRANCE

The first Appellation Controlee of France was first applied in St. Emilion. It was during the English occupation of Bordeaux that the wines of St. Emilion were exposed to the rest of the world. Large shipments were sent to England and this wine was a favorite of many of England's reigning kings, who praised them so much they were always served to visiting rulers. In the year 1199, King John of England signed the Magna Charta and in doing so St. Emilion received its own charter. The ruling town officials, proud of this recognition of their town, applied strict rules and regulations in the making of the wines from St. Emilion. Set into law and regulated by the ruling English monarchs, only a few adjacent hamlets and the village of St. Emilion were allowed to supply England with wines bearing the name Semilione, with a brand on every cask of wine with a coat of arms and recorded in official shipping documents. The official Appellation, instituted in 1955 used the same boundaries of 1199 as the zone for St. Emilion classification.

*Semilione was the English spelling for St. Emilion and not to be confused with the semilione grape grown elsewhere in Bordeaux.

– Thomas Jefferson 1743 – 1826 –

"Wine gives great pleasure and every pleasure is of itself good"

"Claret is a drink for boys, port to men and brandy to heroes"

– Samuel Johnson-British Author – 1709-1784 –

DETERMINING A GOOD VINTAGE

At Chateau La Tour Martillac, a grand cru classe in the Graves region, a story persists about one of the old time workers who had his own way of determining a good vintage. "If the juice from the grapes was sticky enough to glue his hand to his walking cane, a good vintaged wine will be made."

THE SECRET OF CHATEAU MARGAUX

Pierre Ginestet, the previous owner of Chateau Margaux, often relates the tale of how he saved his private reserve of thousands of bottles of wine with some dating back to 1865, from the German occupying forces in the Second World War. They were placed at the end of the huge vat house along with Chateau Lafite's precious reserves and were hidden by huge amounts of empty wooden cases to give the impression to the Germans that nothing of value could possibly be worth the effort to remove that huge pile of discarded wooden boxes. Thus, the valuable wine reserves were saved.

PROTECTION AGAINST DISEASES

Mademoiselle Averous, then owner of Chateau Lynch Bages, during the disastrous Phylloxera plague that devastated all the vines of Europe during the 1880s, was a devoutly religious person. To prevent the phylloxera pest from destroying her precious vines, she placed her faith in religion. She gave casks of wine to the priests of Lourdes, which was just south of Bordeaux. In return, they would return the casks filled with holy water, which she instructed her workers to sprinkle on the vines hoping this would halt the devastation caused by the imported insect from the Eastern United States. Unfortunately, this was to no avail. She eventually had to graft her vines onto American rootstock.

THE FAMILY STRUCTURE OF WINES

A tale overheard by a visitor to France–a visitor was asking a Frenchman to explain the difference between the wines of France since he was confused about the different regions and how or why the wines differed. The old Frenchman wasn't about to go into a long technical explanation. So, he told his inquisitive and confused visitor that French wines are like a family. The Mother was Bordeaux wine – soft, mature, graceful, intelligent and somewhat evasive yet alluring and long lived. The Father was the wines of Burgundy – a little more robust and sturdier, yet still a gentleman. The young Son was Beaujolais – softer, lighter, lacking maturing. The Daughter was the wine of the Loire Valley – young, fragrant, fresh and delicate. Rhone wines were the Uncle and Alsace, the Aunts of the family. All other regions were cousins. After the Frenchman finished his tale, the visitor inquired where did Cognac fit into the family picture. The Frenchman replied that this was the tough old Granddaddy and Champagne was the weddings, birthdays, and all other joyous family events in their life.

NAPOLEON'S FAVORITE WINE

Napoleon was such a great lover of Chambertin wine that even during his retreat from Moscow, he insisted his camp be set up with white linen on his table and he be served his beloved Chambertin, while Marshal Ney, his commander in the field would hold off the advancing Cossacks with a few beaten and frozen troops.

Napoleon is said to have his wine glass designed from a mold of Josephine's breast.

NAKED INDIANS

During the early days when the Spaniards were setting up missionaries in California, along the El Camino Real vineyards were planted with vine cuttings brought from Mexico that had come to Mexico on Spanish Galleons. There was no particular name for the grapes so they called them mission grapes. These made a poor to mediocre wine. The missions lacked proper winemaking equipment or cooperage. A German Jesuit, Jorge Retz solved the problem by hollowing out huge rocks to be used as fermenting vats. Indians did the crushing with their hair tied up and wearing only cloth over their hands to wipe perspiration. After a cleansing bath, they would enter the stone vats and begin to thrash about macerating the grapes. The juices were then transferred into leather bags, which, with some luck, would ferment into wine.

THE SMELL OF A FOX

That "foxy taste" often used in referring to the concord taste in a native Labrusca grape of the east coast was first coined in 1722 by an early American chronicler, Robert Beverly, when he described the grapes of Virginia as having "a rank taste when ripe, resembling the smell of a fox."

"By wine we are generous made;
It furnishes fancy with wings;
Without it we ne'er should have had
Philosophers, poets, or kings.

– Anon.: "Wine and Wisdom" 17 –

"Every time you drink a glass of champagne, Uncle Sam takes a quarter for the privilege."

❧

SWIMMING IN WINE

When a red wine is made, the skin from which the wine attains its red color rises to the top of the vat during fermentation and develops a thick crust. This crust must be broken up to allow the Carbon Dioxide gases to escape. In the Burgundy region of France many years ago, a primitive method was used. Several men would remove all their clothes, climb into the open vat and swim and thrash about to break up the crust until they were exhausted and could no longer stand the suffocating gases. Of course, this practice is no longer used. As an added precaution, workers that were standing guard over the wine swimmers would carry lighted candles as a precautionary measure. If the candles flickered or became dim, this was an indication that the Carbon Dioxide gases were at suffocating level and would tug on the top that was tied to the swimmers ankle as a warning signal, or if the gases overcame the swimmers, he could be removed with the safety rope.

❧

THE HAPPY CARPENTER

In the early 1700s, wine shippers usually hired a carpenter to accompany their convoys of wine being shipped in wooden barrels to repair the kegs at every stop along the way.

❧

WINE, THE ANCIENT MEDICINE

Hippocrates repeatedly insisted upon the virtues of wine as a medicine. It was good for the body and for the mind. Drinking it was as necessary to health and happiness as nutrition, exercise and cleanliness.

略

FOR MAN'S SPIRITUAL HEALTH

The ancient tradition of medicine was kept alive in the West by the church, which propagated the drinking of wine as part of its formula for man's spiritual health. The two principal elements of the church's ritual are bread and wine. Throughout its history, the Catholic Church has never compromised on those two essentials. Some Protestant tavern may have taken to using grape juice in their services, but Catholicism has always insisted upon the fermented juice of the grapes, even in regions where wines cannot be or usually are not made. In parts of tropical Africa, for example, where the traditional drink is palm wine, missionaries have frequently sought permission to use this local beverage in the Eucharist. Such petitions have always been rejected.

略

NAKED NOAH

Yayin was the wine from Noah's vineyard, who, producing and drinking the product, got drunk and was sighted standing naked in his tent.

略

LES GODDAMS

One of the most important acts of French history occurred in the medieval town of Chinon in the heart of the Loire Valley known for its red and Rosè wines. King Charles VII was one of the last holdouts against the English invasion. A young dairymaid from Alsace Lorraine had heard voices that told her to drive the English out of France and crown Charles sat Reims as the King of France. She traveled across France to persuade Charles to accept his destiny. Charles wasn't happy to hear of this girl, named Joan of Arc, and thought she was somewhat crazy. To avoid her, he disguised himself as a courtier and had someone else act the part of King. As Joan entered the city, she immediately singled him out from the crowd and labeled him a coward. Astonished by her ability in finding him, he agreed to equip her with all the horses, men and weapons to drove out "Les Goddams", a favorite description for the hated English. This was the beginning of the dairymaid's courageous battle to recreate the glorious kingdom of France.

LAND OF THE ILL

Alsace got its name from the stream "Ill" – when the Romans first arrived they called the wine growing region, "Land of the Ill" in Latin, Ilsus and from this the name Alsace evolved.

THE STARS OF COGNAC

The practice of awarding stars for Cognac's rating was related to the effects of comets, thus stars were used. The more, the better for the Cognac.

"If God forbade drinking, would he have made wine so good?"

– Armand Cardinal Richelieu –

HE DIED WHISPERING
"COS d'ESTOURNEL 1848"

In Bertall's book *LaVigne*, there is an anecdote about a famous taster. He was primarily a nose and a mouth – he didn't live – he tasted. One day his carriage turned over, and the connoisseur fell out and fractured his skull. His condition was serious and he was carried into a house where the doctor decided to bathe his wound with old wine. The patient was unconscious but as some of the wine trickled down to the corner of his mouth, he suddenly slinked and his lips began to move. Everyone bent forward to hear his dying words. And then came his whispered final verdict on wine, weak and choked: "Cos d'Estournel 1848..." Having correctly identified both the estate and the vintage, the expert died content!

THE WEEPING SPIGOT

Chantepleure is a term used by many French wine makers for the spigot that is inserted into the barrel to draw wine. When the spigot is opened, it makes a singing (chante) sound and when the spigot is closed it sounds like weeping (pleure) thus Chante-pleure.

POMEROL THE FRUIT OF BORDEAUX

When the Romans occupied Bordeaux, they referred to Pomerol as the fruit-growing center and the Latin work for fruit (Pomum) evolved into the name Pomerol.

≥❧

"May our wine brighten the mind and strengthen the resolution."

– Old Saying –

≥❧

"By the bread and salt, by the water and wine,
Thou are welcome, friend, at this board of mine."

– Old English Toast –

≥❧

WARMING OF THE BLOOD

"A good sherris-sack hath a two-fold operation in it. It ascends me into the brain; dries me there all the foolish and dull and crudy vapours which environ it; makes it apprehensive, quick forgetive, full of nimble fiery and delectable shapes, which deliver'd o'er to the voice, the tongue, which is the birth, becomes excellent wit. The second property of your excellent sherris is, the warming of the blood; which, before cold and settled, left the liver white and pale, which is the badge of pusillanimity and cowardice; but the sherris warms it and makes it course from the inwards to the parts extreme. It illumineth the fact, which as a beacon, gives warning to all the rest of this little kingdom, man, to arm; and then the vital commoners and inland petty spirits muster me all to their captain, the heart, who, great and puffed up with this retinue, doth any deed of courage; and this valour comes of sherris. So that skill in the weapon is nothing without sack, for it sets it awork; and learning, a mere hoard of gold kept by a devil till sack commences it and sets it in act and use. Hereof comes it that Prince Harry is valiant; for the cold blood he did naturally inherit of his father, he hath, like lean, sterile, and bare land, manured, husbanded, and tilled, with excellent endeavour of drinking good and good store of fertile sherris, that he is become very hot and valiant. If I had a thousand sons, the first human principle I would teach them should be, to forswear this potations and to addict themselves to sack.

– Sir John Falstaff –

14

"Wine drunken with moderation is the joy of the soul and the Heart", from the book of aprochylia 180 B.C.

SPANISH MOORS DISCOVERED DISTILLATION

The Moors of Spain are generally credited with having discovered the secret of distillation, despite their religious rule of abstinence. That they did not simply make Sherry to sell to the infidels is patent in the records. A variety of dodges were invented to get around the tenets of the Koran. In Cordoba, for example, an inebriated Moor was brought before the Chief Kadi. A court official, employed for the purpose, was asked to determine whether the accused's breath smelled of wine. The reply saved everybody's face. While the man's breath smelled, he said who could tell whether it was grape juice or wine. Case dismissed.

A HALF-PENNY WORTH OF BREAD

"O monstrous! but one half-pennyworth of bread to this intolerable deal of Sack!" exclaimed Prince Hal, having seen Falstaff's huge bill at the Boar's Head Tavern for gallons of Sherry and a bit of bread. Falstaff's reply, rather than an apology, constituted one of his many odes to Sherry.

֍

"Good wine is an aid to digestion and a promoter of good cheer. I don't think anyone will find a sound argument against the moderate use of it."

– George Ade –

֍

"Then let us drink old sacke, boyes,
Which makes us fond and merry,
The life of mirth and joy on earth,
Is a cuppe of good old sherry."

– Anon., 17ᵗʰ century poet –

֍

GUARDING VINEYARDS AND DAUGHTERS

Spaniards have a saying: "It is difficult to guard vineyards and daughters." When it comes to vineyards, they try hard. They post a man day and night in a vienteveo, a little sentry hut on stilts, to protect the grapes from marauding animals and people.

֍

"I sometimes think that never blows so red the rose as where some buried Caesar bled."

– Omar Khayyam describing wines of the Cotê de Nuits –

❧

"Wine is one of the noblest cordials in nature."

– British preacher and founder of Methodism, Sept. 1771 –

❧

DYING BEFORE THE AGE OF 90

In Jerez, there is a saying that anyone dying before the age of 90 has gone in his infancy. To back up the claim, a study of the families operating the great Sherry bodegas of Spain – all ardent devotees of their products – revealed that only 10% died before the age of 70, and 15% lived beyond 90.

❧

THE MEDICINAL BENEFITS OF WINE

Dr. Alexander Flemming, on a visit to Jerez, is said to have exclaimed, "Penicillin may cure the sick, but this Sherry could bring a dead man back to life."

Another Spanish claim is that Sherry in half bottles was introduced so that everyone could drink at his own pace. Individuality of person is as revered as individuality of Sherries.

❧

SINGEING THE KING'S BEARD

Legend has it that Sir Francis Drake lived in Cadiz when a young man. One day in a public argument, he was struck down. Infuriated by this outrageous insult, he departed Spain. In 1587, the Englishman got his revenge by "singeing the beard of the King of Spain" – burning the Spanish fleet as it lay anchored in Cadiz Bay. Carrying retaliation to the final degree, he stole, and carried off to England, 3,000 casks of Sherris-Sack.

THE FRAUD BRIGADE

France has a special wine police Bureau called "La Brigade pour la Prevention de la Fraud" (The Brigade for the Prevention of Fraud) that has absolute police power concerning wine trade and anyone connected with it.

ℰ

"Wine gives strength to weary men."

– Homer–

ℰ

"Who prates of war or want after taking wine."

– Horace 65 B.C. –

ℰ

NAPOLEON BONAPARTE
THE FATHER OF SHERRY

Napoleon Bonaparte was responsible for the discovery of Sherry. In 1798, he invaded Egypt and as was the custom, his troops were issued a daily ration of wine. The temperature in Egypt was a constant reading of 90°-110° and this high heat was spoiling the wine. His troops began to be disgruntled, so Napoleon, who was famous for the statement "an army travels on its stomach," had to find a solution to this problem. After consulting with his staff, the problem was corrected by adding Brandy to the wine to act as a preservative and thus evolved "fortification," the process used in making Sherry today.

HENRY THE IV'S START IN LIFE

In the pleasant wine region of Juracon in the southeast of France is the place where the king of Navarre is said to have moistened the lips of his son, the future Henry IV with wine and garlic to develop a taste for gastronomy and great wine.

A man who was fond of wine was offered some grapes at dessert after dinner. "Much obliged," he said, pushing the plate to one side. "I am not accustomed to taking my wine in pills."

– Brillat Savarin –

SHERRY WITH BREAKFAST

Thomas Randolph wrote in praise of Sherry: We care not for money, riches or wealth. Old Sack is our money, Old Sack is our wealth.

In the old days, the Sherry families moved to a house right on the vineyards for the period of the harvest. The heads of these families believed that a breakfast of one or two glasses of Cream Sherry, fried bread and hot chocolate would give them the endurance and strength for the long hard day's work.

WATER THE BULLRING

In Jerez, there is a custom called <u>regar la plaza</u> – to water the bullring. In Sanlucar de Barrameda, the local idiom translates to "prepare the bed." In both cities, it refers to the custom of serious drinkers who invariably start their day with a sweet, rich Oloroso Cream to provide a stomach liner for the many Finos to follow.

"Now keep ye from the white and from the red,
And namely from the white wine of Lepe,
This is to sell in Fish Street or in Chepe.
This wine of Spain creepeth subtilly
In other wines, growing fast by,
Of which there riseth such fumositee,
That when a man hath drunken draughts three,
And weneth that he be at home in Chepe,
He is in Spain, right at the town of Lepe,
Not at the Rochelle, nor at Bordeaux town."

– Chaucer, "Pardoner's Tale" –

PROTECTING SHERRY WITH BREAD

Tapas is the Spanish equivalent of canapés or hors d'oeuvres, although the custom has grown to include an extensive buffet of hot and cold dishes in many instances.

The time of origin of tapas is lost, but the stories of how they came into being are not. It seems that in the warm climate of southwestern Spain where Sherry is produced, the proprietor of a local tavern decided to protect the region's liquid gold by placing a piece of bread on top of the mini tulip glass (copita) in which it was served. His reason was simply to protect the wine from the inevitable buzzing insects with a cover. The Spanish word for cover is tapa. Inevitably, the bread was eaten by the customer.

Other cafes and taverns followed suit, until one more enterprising than the rest placed a small glass dish atop the copita and filled it with tidbits of pungent ripe and stuffed green olives, a few of the marvelous seafoods for which the region is noted, albondigas (Spanish meatballs), salted nuts and the like. Thus was born the term tapas to describe these foods.

The first offering of tapas is free, which in no time at all led to the custom the Spaniards call chateo – or bar-hopping. Americans stationed at the region's missile base in Rota call it tapa-hopping. As Americans are unused to the typically late Spanish dinner hour (anywhere from 10:00 P.M. to midnight), they are said to indulge in a lot of tapa-hopping to fill the void.

The Roman Martial (A.D. 43-104) was credited with the following lines:

Three Cups for Amy
Four to Kate to be given
To Susan, five, six Rachel
Bridget, seven.

LICKING WINDOW PANES

The Danish prince, Aage once made the statement that "an evening of drinking champagne was like an evening spent rushing from house to house licking dusty window panes.

કર્

CONCORD, MASSACHUSETTS

The first planting of the Concord grape was planted by Ephraim Bull in 1843 at Concord, Massachusetts.

કર્

AN ARCHEOLOGIST'S DISCOVERY

A team of Archeologists discovered a Royal Egyptian tomb that had been plundered of its treasure. Within the tomb they found two empty wine jars that had been opened and had been drunk by the thieves. On one of the amphorea's was scratched: "this one contains the best wine."

કર્

TEN PERCENT OF SCHLOSS JOHANNISBERG

The famous castle of Schloss Johannisberg sits on a high terrace overlooking the German Rhine River. The wine produced from its vineyards is acclaimed worldwide. In the latter part of the eighteenth century, the estate was seized from its owner, the Church, and was given over to Prince Metternich as a reward for his service and diplomacy when he presided at the Vienna Congress in 1814. The Austrian Emperor did so with a condition that he was to receive ten percent of the vineyard's production annually. The present owner of Schloss Johannisberg still pays the levy in money, not in wine.

THE MANY NAMES OF PORT

Ever wonder how the different names associated with port wine from Oporto, Portugal like Director's Port, Partner's Port, Manager's Port, Club Port, etc. came about? In the city of Oporto is an English Club called the Factory House. Weekly luncheons are held by English firms in the trade of Port wines. Directors of the company are served the best port, called Director's Port. Partner's port is served at the Wine Trade Club in London for members of the branches of the firms and Manager's Port is reserved strictly for the managers of the various branches of the firm.

WINE IN KING TUT'S TOMB

Much was made about the great discoveries of gold in King Tutankhamen's tomb. Very little was mentioned about the wine jars that were discovered in the young king's tomb in 1922. Tutankhamen died in the year 1352 B.C. The wine jars were sealed, but, of course, no wine remained, only residual powder. Other royal tombs were raided and plundered in ancient times and some archaeologists have discovered messages on wine jars written by the robbers, such as, "This one contains the best wine."

❧

"No poem was ever written by a drinker of water."

– Horace (65 B.C.) –

❧

"Wine to the poet is a winged steed;
Those who drink water gain but little speed."

– Nicaentus, c. 250 B.C. –

❧

"I often wonder what the vintners buy
One half so precious as the stuff they sell."

– Omar Khayyàm: (? – 1123) –

❧

LUXEMBOURG WATER

The vineyards of Luxembourg are situated in many villages along the upper Mosel. One of the best wines comes from the town of Wasserbillig, which means "cheap water".

೨ಲ

A CUP OF SACK

Sparkling wines are called "sekt" in Germany. Ludwig Devrient, who played a role in Shakespeare's Henri IV, knew nothing about sparkling wines. He would often visit his favorite weinstobe and call for a cup of sack (sekt) and the name stuck. Since 1815, German sparkling wines have been called "Sekt".

೨ಲ

COLD DUCK

Kalte Ente, Cold Duck, is believed to have originated in Germany. Kalte Ente in German means cold ends. After a night of drinking, all the remaining wine was gathered and blended together and sparkling wine was added for a night cap for the remaining hearty drinkers to the end of the night of drinking. A visiting restaurant owner from Detroit had sampled the concoction and liked it so well, he began serving it in his restaurant but his mixture was somewhat different. He blended a New York State white champagne with a sparkling red. From California, the popularity grew rapidly and in Michigan in 1960, the marketing of the sparkling blend under the name Cold Duck was begun.

THE SOAKED OAK

cartoon

THE SOAKED OAK

Behind the old Rhine house at the Beringer winery in the Napa Valley of California stands an old oddly shaped oak tree which has a large trunk with crooked and spirally branches that twist and turn in an unusual form. How this came about is an interesting tale. Back in the time when the two Beringer Brothers started making wine, they stored some red wine in an old storage shed that housed a large wooden cask and periodically they would check the development of the wine. To their surprise, the wine level of the cask was receding rapidly, more than could be allowed for evaporation. The brothers concluded that a thief was at work, probably during the late night hours. It was then decided that each of the brothers would take turns and stand guard at night with a shotgun to apprehend the thief. Still the wine was disappearing, and each one would accuse the other of falling asleep during his vigil. It wasn't until the old storage house and wooden cask were dismantled to make room for the buildings that were to be erected as the winery increased in size, that workmen discovered that the roots of the oak tree had found their way under the old wooden cask and were absorbing wine through separation in the wood. Tour guides at the winery related this tale and refer to the happy looking tree as the "soaked oak".

TEN VINES FOR EVERY INDIAN

The first vines planted in the new world were in Mexico, not California. Cortez was the ruler and he ordered all Spanish grant holders to plant vines, ten for every Indian living on the land, for five years running. This plan eventually failed and the vines were transported into California when the first missions were founded at Loreto at the end of the seventeenth century.

THE ELEPHANT WINE

Some Wurtemburg wines are referred to as elephant wine because the grapes are so hard that it would take an elephant to crush them. Germany, like many other nations, does not use the word champagne on their sparkling wines. The work "Sekt" is used instead. It is believed to originate back to the year 1815 to Lord Ludwig Devrient who played Shakespeare's Henry IV and after every performance would stop in his local weinstube and would call for a cup of sack (sekt), a local wine that had a little sparkle to it, and the name stuck.

LIEBFRAUMILCH

Worms, the historical town in the Rheinhessen wine district in the Rhine region of Germany, is also responsible for the world famous Liebfraumilch. The church of Our Lady or Liebfrauenkirche has a vineyard in front of the church that is enclosed within the church property. The vineyard is the Liebfrauenstift and there are many different stories about the origin of Liebfraumilch for the last part of the name "milch" means "monk" in German but over the years since the 1700s the meaning was somewhat changed to the word for "milk" which does not mean milk in German. Originally, it was the wine of Our Lady "Liebfrau" made by the monks "milch" who served the church. But folklore has changed it to Our Lady's Milk. However, the popular Liebfraumilch of today does not come from this small particular vineyard but from the entire Rheinhessen region. The wine that is produced from this particular vineyard is labeled "Liebfrauenstift", which is not of any particular quality, indeed a plain wine.

PLANTING VINES TO AVOID A FINE

In the Middle Ages, the peasants in the Veneto region of Italy were required to plant a required number of new vines each year or pay a heavy fine.vines planted in lava

VINES PLANTED IN LAVA

On the Sicilian island of Pantelleria, the soil is volcanic. To grow vines, farmers have to dig holes in the lava and put the vine cutting together with some soil. Until the vine has taken hold, it must be watered by hand. Finally, the roots grow and split the lava and the plant is able to survive, then the vine is protected from the scorching winds with a silo-like structure built of rocks.

THE FOOTPRINT OF SARDINIA

A mark of the Divine on the land and its wines – In ancient times, Sardinia was called Ichnusa from the Greek Ichnos, for footprint. The Greeks were convinced that the shape was no accident but dated to the time of creation. They said that the Creator, when his work was almost done, lumped together what earth was left over and plopped it down in the middle of the Mediterranean and stomped it down with his foot.

SOAVE, A PLACE OF GREAT SUAVITY

Soave is one of the famous white wines of Italy. The name comes from the ancient town of Suave in the Val Tramigna. It derives according to the most credited hypothesis, from the Latin Sauvium, for the land of the Suevi or Soavi, a barbarian people who conquered the region in 568 A.D.

THE LEGEND OF CHATEAU RAUZAN GASSIES

There is a persistent tale often repeated to visitors in the parish of Margaux in the Haut Medoc region of Bordeaux about Chateau Rauzan Gassies 2nd Grand Cru Classe. This is one of the owners back in the early 1800s that had a liking for birds and always resisted advice to cut the tree line down at the rear of the estate to take advantage of the easterly prevailing winds that carried the moisture from the Atlantic Ocean. He, of course, insisted that the trees remain so his beloved feathered friends would have a place to nest and raise their young. The tale goes on to tell that the birds were grateful for this consideration and when the vineyard was threatened with a devastating hail storm, the birds would perch on the vines and protect the precious berries with their wings.

THIRTY CASKS OF CLOS VOUGEOT

The wines of Burgundy were famous and sought after as long as a thousand years ago. During the middle ages, most of the great wines of Burgundy were reserved strictly for the Royalty. Pope Gregory XI awarded the position of Cardinal to any priest who would send him "thirty casks of Clos Vougeot".

MY HEART IS AT CALON

The label of Chateau Calon Segur, a grand cru in St. Estephe always has an outline of a heart of the label that encases the name of the Chateau. This dates back two centuries when the Marquis Alexandre de Segur owned the wine estates including Chateau Lafite and was reported to make the statement, "I made wine at Lafite, but my heart is at Calon."

➴

Wine is mentioned 165 times in the Bible.

➴

THE HERMIT VINEYARDS

As one would assume, the vineyards of Hermitage are named after a Hermit. After the holy war, a crusader wanting to escape from realities and cruelties of the harsh world settled in a secluded site on a mountain top overlooking the Rhone Valley. He wanted to plant vines but the soil was too rocky. He broke the large rocks into small pebbles so the vines would have a chance to grow but this failed. To compensate for all the killing he inflicted on other people during the war, he made up for this by being kind to animals. One evening, the weather was very harsh and stormy, so he gathered all the animals and provided them with shelter in his meager hut. An angel who had observed this act of kindness shed a tear that fell on the hermit's vines and from that time on, they flourished along with any other vines the hermit would plant.

➴

THE TERRIBLE WINES OF BORDEAUX

Before the 1600s Bordeaux was an area or district where King Louis XIII would send members of his court in punishment. The King thought that Bordeaux wines were terrible. One such member was Richelieu and his friends tricked the King by substituting a Bordeaux wine for his favorite Burgundy. While in Bordeaux, Richelieu discovered some great wines of that region and when his punishment was over, he returned to the King's court and began to spread the word of his great find and by his efforts the fame of Bordeaux grew rapidly.

ن

"If you are selling wine, serve cheese. If you are buying wine, eat apples" is an old saying among wine producers in France.

ن

WHERE NAPOLEON FAILED,
CHATEAU HAUT BRION SUCCEEDED

Chateau Haut Brion, one of the five premier grand crus of 1855 is the only great estate owned by an American. Clarence Dillon, former treasurer of the United States and father of Douglas Dillon, former Ambassador to France, is the owner.

One of its former owners was Talleyrand, Napoleon's Foreign Minister. During the French Revolution, Talleyrand was sent as a representative of France after her defeat to face the conquering nations of Prussia, Austria and England. Talleyrand was a gourmet so he had Careme, one of France's greatest chefs, accompany him and the French Government shipped cases of his famous Chateau Haut Brion wine to the congress of Vienna where the fate of defeated France was to be determined. Talleryrand had another talent of being very witty and a good conversationalist and outstanding social charm. With his combination of gourmet food prepared by France's greatest chef and the superb Haut Brion wine and his silver tongue, he soon turned the boring negotiations into a social gathering of the highest caliber. He left Vienna with more territory for France than it owned before the war. Where Napoleon failed, Talleyrand succeeded with Chateau Haut Brion and Careme, the gourmet chef.

જ્છ

THE LONE TOWER OF CHATEAU LATOUR

The famous tower on the label of Chateau Latour is all that remains of an original Chateau that was owned by an English sympathizer during the war between England and France. The French ruler ordered the Chateau destroyed and the towers cut off, saying that this would happen to the traitor's head if he ever caught up with him. All that is left today is the one lone tower. The sympathizer was never caught.

જ્છ

A DONKEY STARTED
THE PRACTICE OF PRUNING

France, being a religious country, had many saints and one traveled with a donkey. One day St. Martin made a visit in one of the vineyards in Burgundy and the tale is told that he tied his donkey to some vines while he visited with his Vigneron friend. When the visit was over, the vineyard owner and St. Martin walked to where the donkey was tied up and discovered the mule ate all the leaves within his reach. The Vigneron and St. Martin had to clip the vines. This infuriated the vine grower so that he never forgot the incident throughout the year. To his surprise, when the next yield was harvested, he discovered the grapes from the vines, which had some of the leaves eaten by the donkey, produced a higher grade of wine. It was from this event that pruning was first discovered in the development of better fruit.

❧

ROADSIDE TAVERN NOW A FAMOUS CHATEAU

The famous Chateau, Cheval Blanc, one of the first growths of St. Emilion, was first a post house where horses could be changed. Henry IV had stopped there to change horses and he always insisted on white horses. This was on the road from Paris to Pau and from these visits from this famous person, the inn was called Chaval Blanc and was later transformed into a wine chateaux.

❧

"How goes the time? 'Tis five o'clock, go fetch a pint of port."

– *Author unknown* –

❧

"I AM DRINKING STARS"

Dom Perignon was placed in charge of the wine cellars at the Abbey of Haut Villiers in 1660. He loved his work dearly and was always looking for ways to improve the wine-making process and its equipment. One problem that could not be solved by his predecessors for a thousand years was air that came in contact with the wine and caused rapid spoilage. Some of the methods used to prevent this were rolled up grapevine leaves, inserted into the bottle neck. This failed because the second fermentation in the bottle would force the stopper out. Oil soaked rags, olive oil poured on top of the wine, were two other methods that failed. When the wine was bottled in fall and rested through the winter, the following spring was when the remaining sugar would start to referment, causing carbon dioxide gases to build within the bottle (of course, this process was unknown). Dom Perignon began to putter with different devices. He tried wooden stoppers but the fit wasn't perfect and wine would seep out. He finally used cork, and when he opened his bottle, the cork "popped". When he drank some of the wine to test its quality, he shouted, "I am drinking stars!"

CHAMPAGNE BARREL RACE

Every year on June 24th, St. John's Day, the coopers hold an annual barrel race in the champagne district in the town of Ay. Coopers from the many champagne houses are invited to compete. The cellar workers race by rolling the huge casks down narrow streets with only the tip of their forefingers to guide them. The frequent winners are the team from the Bollinger firm and proudly so, since it is Madam Bollinger who awards the silver cup to the winners.

WINE OF THE DEVIL

Before Dom Perignon refined the Champagne process to control the carbon dioxide gases with second fermentation in the bottle and the cork enclosure, the wine makers referred to the wine as "Vin Diable" (wine of the devil). When the wine was bottled and laid to rest through the winter, come spring the corks would blow and the bottles would break. The wine makers were confused and bewildered by this happening and some claimed it was the work of the devil, while others thought it was the phase of the moon. Some concluded that it was some sort of mystery connected with the flow of sap of the vines in spring. And the more scientific people blamed the chalk in the soil. Today, champagne is still made by Dom Perignon's process.

The vineyards of Marne in the Champagne district of France were occupied by the Romans in early 80 A.D. They tended and developed the vines to such a degree of quality that the Emperor Domitian in A.D. 92 ordered all the vineyards to be destroyed because they posed a threat to the wines of Italy. However, several centuries later another emperor order the vines replanted.

"Champagne gives brilliance to the eye without flushing the face."

– Madam de Parabere –

"A cavalier may appropriately offer, at propitious intervals, a glass now and then to his danceress. There it takes a fitting rank and position amongst feathers, gauzes, lace, embroidery, ribbons, white satin shoes, and eau-de-cologne, for champagne is simply one of the elegant extras of life.

– Charles Dickens –

THE CHAMPAGNE HEAD STONE

Wealthy James McMillan Gibson was such a great lover of French champagne that he left instructions in his will to have two Nebuchadnezzer (a huge bottle containing the equal of 20 ordinary bottles of champagne) placed atop his grave with one at this feet and one at his head. When he died in Palm Springs in 1966, his wishes were carried out. They remained in this position until the cemetery authorities had them removed. The three feet tall bottles drew a steady stream of the curious and resulted in trampled flowers and scoffed turf. The huge champagne bottles not stand in the widow's garden as a testimony of his love for champagne.

THE GREAT WINE OF THE WESTERN WORLD

Great Western winery of New York State received its name from the French sampling some of their champagnes. The French exclaimed, "A great wine from the Western world, thus Great Western."

THE "LADY JOAN" BOTTLE

A demijohn is an oversized bottle of from one to ten gallons of wine in capacity and is also used to refer to large bottles of champagne. The name is an anglicized word from the French term of Dame Jeanne meaning "Lady Joan".

Sir George Etherege spoke of champagne in a rhyme, "It quickly recovers, poor languishing lovers, makes us frolic and gay and drowns all sorrow, but alas, we relapse again on the morrow."

&

"This wine is full of gases, which to me are offensive, it pleases all you asses, because it is expensive.

– A. P. Herbert, about champagne –

&

THE LOWEST VINEYARD OF THE WORLD

The world's lowest vineyards are in Holland; Piet Hillebrand is Holland's first wine grower. He recently planted about an acre and a half that is 15 feet below sea level about 50 miles northeast of Amsterdam.

&

COMMITING SUICIDE WITH GRAPES

In Persia, an old tale is still repeated to this day that the birth of wine was discovered in the Far East. King Jamshid's harem favorite was a woman named Gulnare who devoured a plate of fermented grapes in order to do away with herself because she was cast aside. Her despair disappeared and the king was so pleased with her discovery that he clasped her to his bosom.

જી

POURING WINE ON THE GROUND
TO PLEASE THE GODS

Nomadic tribesmen who were successful in a hunt would celebrate with a festival and during the celebration, they would sprinkle wine on the ground to receive a blessing from the gods for more successful hunts.

જી

THE IMMORTAL CHINESE WINE

Grapes were planted in China since the dawn of mankind, until they were destroyed by an imperial order over a thousand years ago. Before that, the Chinese made scented wines from rice and the best was called Mandarin and was reserved for the emperor for it was believed that Mandarin was supposed to make one immortal. A court servant stole some of the emperor's wine and was caught and sentenced to death for this unthinkable deed, but the servant was spared when he said, "If Mandarin made him immortal, then death was impossible, and if not, such a crime was not worthy of the penalty," and he was released.

THE TROJAN HORSE OF WINE

In the year 1200, the city of Trier on the Moselle River was part of the ruins of the Roman Empire. Archbishop John I held a great deal of power granted to him by the Vatican. He used his power to control his thriving little bailiwick.

His closest neighbor was Count Frederick of Vianden who had built himself a castle with fortified ramparts which overlooked the city of Trier and who also defied the bishop's attempt to unify the whole country. Count Frederick repulsed all attacks by the Bishop warrior.

Bishop John realized that this approach was useless against the well-built fortress. So another method was needed since he had acquired many acres of vineyards while he was building his little empire which included the famous properties of St. Maximn, Purim and Himmerod. His purple nose was a testimony to his fondness of the grape and he knew the power of wine. He organized a convoy of horses and carts with huge barrels of some of his best wine and then instructed his brave warriors to launch an attack on the solidly built fortress of Count Frederick. As this garrison headed bravely up the hill toward the main gate of the fortress, Count Frederick launched a counter-attack. The door of the fortress flung open and wild, crazed warriors rushed out at the meager band of the Bishop's men who saw they were outnumbered and simply abandoned the assault and hid in the woods and bushes, leaving the wagons of precious wine. Frederick's troops, discovered the great prize they had conquered, drove the wine into the fortress, where a celebration went on all night. They consumed the precious wine and everyone feasted – men, women and even children. At dawn, the Bishop made his move, it took only minutes to finish what the wine had started. As Count Frederick's flock awoke.

CAVE DWELLERS DRANK WINE

It is not known when man discovered that the juice of the grape, if allowed to ferment, becomes wine. However, what is known is that the Neolithic man, turning from hunting to agriculture, let his crops ferment, and that people in various parts of the earth learned that grapes (or wet grain), allowed to stand in warmth, became a liquor that possessed strange and pleasant effect. It is possible that a cave dweller who had gathered wild grapes to use their sweet juice as a thirst quencher returned from a hunting trip, picked up the container which he had left, and discovered, that the grape juice had become a different beverage.

CHAMPAGNE AND PHYSICAL EFFICIENCY

Wine can increase the physical efficiency of the organism. Take the case of the famous French cyclist Jacque Anquetil, who used to fill his "water flask" when he was taking on the Pyrenees and the Dolomites with genuine champagne.

– written by Dr. Roberto Morgante in December issue of
Italian Wines and Spirits –

TRADING SLAVES FOR WINE

Traces of the first attempts at prohibition have been found in Romania, once occupied by the Dacians and even in Gaul, where men were forbidden to plant vines. So wine was imported from Italy and other nearby wine producing regions. Prices on the black market were exorbitant – one whole slave being paid for a single amphora of wine.

"Five qualities there in wine's praise advancing:
Strong, beautiful, fragrant, cool and dancing."

– John Harrington:
"The Englishman's Doctor" 1608 –

৯৯

THE SCOTTISH JUDGE AND PORT WINE

Ernest Cockburn wrote of a tale in his book, Port Wine and Oporto, from his great-grandfather's memoirs, who was a Scottish judge, and was accustomed to having bottles of port and biscuits on the bench to sustain him in long sessions:

> The refreshment was generally allowed to stand untouched, as if despised, for a short time during which their Lordships seemed to be intent only on their notes. But in a little while, some water was poured into a tumbler and sipped quietly, as if merely to sustain nature. Then a few drops of wine were ventured upon but only with the water; till at last patience could endure no longer and a full bumper of the pure black element was tossed over; after which the thing went on regularly and there was a comfortable munching and quaffing to the great envy of the parched throats in the gallery.

৯৯

FOG WINE

The Nebbiolo, which derives its name from the Italian work "nebbia", meaning mist or fog, comes from the autumn, when the hills of the Langhe region of Piedmont in northeast Italy are shrouded in misty, morning fogs.

"O beatific Burgundy, well may be called the mother of men whose breasts give such wonderful milk."

– Erasmus –

"Wine drunk with moderation is the joy of the soul and the heart."

– written in a book of the Apocrypha, 180 B.C. –

George, Duke of Clarence (1449-1478), a younger of Edward IV, is said to have drowned in a butt of Malmsey wine.

There is a sturdy red wine produced in the Lombardy region of Italy called Sangue di Guida, which means "Blood of Judas".

SILK STOCKINGS AND DEER

Bill Wagner, owner of Wagner vineyard in Lodi, New York on the eastern shore of one of the Finger Lakes in New York State, relates the story of how he controls the deer menace. This plagues his vineyards. By placing human hair in silk stockings sporadically among his vines, he discourages the invasion of the deer. He also notes that a telltale sign that raccoons visited his vineyard, is the pits found on the ground. It seems raccoons love grapes but not the seeds.

47

WINE AND THE MINE

The popular California Almaden winery was named after the quicksilver mine in the Santa Cruz Mountains which was named by the early Spanish explorers Al-maden, meaning mine.

A BIT OF PARIS IN CALIFORNIA

Louis Benoist, the last private owner of the Almaden vineyards, before its purchase by National Distillers, would entertain his guests in a specially built French café in the basement of his residence. Every detail and décor was painstakingly reproduced to give one the feeling he was truly back in a Paris café during the 1800s. Monsieur Benoist would not allow any electric lighting fixtures in his dining room. At each evening meal, the room was illuminated with new candles at a cost of approximately $30.00 to $40.00.

"May friendship, like wine, improve as time advances."

– *Old English Toast* –

"May our love be like good wine, grow stronger as it grows older."

– Old English Toast –

෨ළ

CHATEAU DE LA MOTHE

Chateau Margaux, one of the most famous of the First Growths, is one of the oldest estates of the Medoc dating back to the fifteenth century, and was previously called Chateaux de la Mothe.

෨ළ

A PRISONER VISITS HIS FORMER CAPTOR

During the Second World War, when the allied forces retook Bordeaux, some of the German prisoners were used at Chateau Beausejour to build a small tower. After the war, the tower had to be removed for a new vat house to be built. The exact day the tower was being dismantled, one of the German prisoners who had worked on building the tower was touring St. Emilion and stopped at the chateau. M. Becot welcomed him and his family and he has photographs of the German showing his family where he had engraved his name on a rock during the war with his fellow prisoners at Chateau Beausejour.

When the English rule of Bordeaux ended in 1453, France looked upon the area as an occupation zone. Fearing that the subjects would still be loyal to the English crown, two forts were built to guard it and the inhabitants. When the King of France was informed that the Forts were finished, lacking something royal to say, he just muttered Ha! So, one fort was named Chateau Ha. It no longer exists today.

෨ළ

"Bring me a flagon, Enough for a Dragon, and fill it with Chateau Yguem."

– A.P. Herbert in the song "Table for Tw

❧

"When childless families despair, when January is wedded to May, and when old men wish to be young then Tokay is in request."

– Morton P. Shand quotes of an Englishman –

❧

TREATING WOUNDS WITH WINE

The Greek physician Mnesitheus said of wine, "in medicine it is most beneficial... while dark wine is most favorable to bodily growth, white wine is thinnest and most diuretic; yellow wine is dry, and better adapted to digesting foods."

❧

VINEYARDS IN NEW YORK CITY

Around 1750 wine grapes were growing in what is now Flushing on Long Island. The believe it or not, grapevines grew in New York City in the mid-1800s, though few are aware that the "Big Apple" might have been known as the Big Grape then.

GEORGE WASHINGTON, THE FATHER OF MADEIRA

The father of our country, George Washington, enjoyed a glass or two of Madeira with his evening meal. The early colonists came to love Madeira. By an oversight, King Charles II decided that the island of Madeira was not part of Europe and he allowed the wine to arrive duty free in America, but only on American ships. All other goods shipped from Europe were to be detoured through England where English duty and freight charges were added.

HAVE A GLASS OF SHERRY

In Spain, they never say "have another glass of sherry", but say "Have a glass of sherry" for each glass is a discovery; nor do they say the glass of sherry but Penultina copa, the next-to-the-last glass for there should be no end of such a good thing.

"Wine refreshes the stomach, sharpens the appetite, blunts care and sadness, and conduces to slumber."

– Plin –

GETTING FOXED

"Getting foxed" was a term used by the colonists for getting tipsy.

FOR THE GLORY OF THE CHURCH

Dante, in the Divina Commedia, consigned Pope Martin IV (1281-1285), a Frenchman from Tours, to Purgatory for his habit of gorging himself on the eels of Lake Bolsena drowned in Vernaccia. Dante, who referred to the Pope as Simone de Brion, wrote:

"...he had eels taken from the lake of Viterbo (Bolsena) and had them drowned in the wine of Vernaccia, then roasted, he ate them, and he was so pleased by those morsels that he continued to crave them and had them slaughtered and drowned in his chambers, and about the fact of drink he had not style nor limits and when he was well waxed, he would say: "Oh, good God, what pain we suffer for the glory of the Church!"

COOKING SHERRY

The term cooking sherry is said to originate in England back in the early 1800s when the wealthy and prominent people would send to Spain for their sherry supply. The drinking sherry was stored in separate quarters, and the low-grade sherry used for cooking was usually stored in the kitchen. But many of the household servants would help themselves to a glass of sherry and the supply would quickly dwindle. So the master of the house would add salt to the wine to make it somewhat undrinkable and would stamp across the face of the barrel "cooking sherry" which was to discourage the house servants from drinking the unpalatable wine whereas salt was always used in cooking and would not affect the wine's purpose.

THE SAD BIRD OF THE LOIRE VALLEY

Legend has it that the nightingale bird first sang somewhere on the Loire Valley many years ago. The nightingale was a silent and sad bird because it had only one eye and could not see all the beauty of the Loire. A worm encountered the lonely and sad bird and asked why it was silent and depressed. The nightingale told the worm it had only one eye. The worm, taking pity, lent the bird one of her eyes, declaring it would be better to see all the beauty of the Loire with two eyes and she only needed one to dig holes in the soil. Throughout the night, the bird sang with happiness. When the worm asked for her eye back, the nightingale refused and soon fell asleep under a vine. The vine took pity on the worm and sent a tendril out to the bird's throat, wrapping around it several times. The nightingale began choking and thought the worm had caught her. She struggled loose and flew to a tree. She swore that she would never sleep again. So today, the worm has only one eye, the vines continue to grow in search of the bird, and sleepless nightingales sing all night.

VOUVRAY, THE PASSPORT TO HEAVEN

Vouvray was called "Le Vin de Curé" by the Belgians in the early 18th century. It was believed the best way to guarantee one's way to heaven was to keep the local priest well supplied with wine.

The Loire River is called the "Smile of France."

"Wine rejoices the heart of man, and joy is the mother of all virtue."

– J. W. Goethe –

THE DAUGHTERS OF COTE du RHONE

Many years ago, a nobleman had two daughters. One had beautiful golden hair and a smile brighter than the sun. The other daughter had black, glossy hair. The father loved each equally. The castle where he lived with his beautiful daughters was surrounded with bountiful vineyards on the banks of the Rhone River. He soon grew old and knew his time on earth would be short. He drew up his will, giving one half of his vineyards to one daughter and the other half to the other daughter. The blonde daughter's vineyard always ripened early. She had married a crusader who died in battle and her beauty soon faded. The dark-haired daughter's vineyards matured slowly and she became the favorite of the king, whom she married.

Today the two main sections are referred to as the Cote Blonde, whose wines mature early but fade soon. The wines of Cote Brune are much different and take longer to mature, but reach a flavor worthy of kings.

🙞

A CURE FOR A HANGOVER

A famous cure for a hangover in Burgundy is a mixture of one ounce of Cassis in a tall glass filled with white Burgundy wine. This drink is called Rince Cochon (rinsed pig).

🙞

Quote of a buyer in Beadna: "Beware of a Burgundian bearing bouillon. He's trying to make you buy a bad Beaume."

🙞

The first region of France to come under the Aypelation d'Origine laws was Chateauneuf de Pape.

રે

WELCOME BASTARD

The world famous "Montrachet" vineyard in the cote du Beaune region of Burgundy which experts claim as the finest white wine produced in the world, has an interesting story related to the vineyards that are attached to it or in close proximity. These small plots or vineyards are called "clos" meaning walled-in sections or separate plots belonging to an individual. At one time in years past, these plots were given specific names and how these titles evolved is unique, to say the least. Before the French Revolution, the Hierarchy of the church and the Dukes of the French Court owned many of the great vineyards in the Burgundy region. After the Revolution, a lot of the large vineyards were to be divided among the people. The owner of the classic Montrachet vineyards had children and he was allowed to give parcels to his descendents. The father would give a name to each of the "clos" or sections with a title befitting their respective traits, personalities, or titles they held. 'Clos les Chevaliers' was named for a son who was an officer in Franc's famous Chevalier's regiment. Another clos was named 'Les Pucelles' for his daughters who never married and the word Pucelles in French means Virgin.

The youngest son was the black sheep of the family. He spent most of his time in Paris enjoying the good life, drinking and keeping company with the fast ladies of the night. To keep as much of his land holdings among the family, he sectioned a parcel of his vineyard and to show his disgust for the life his son was leading, he named that particular clos "Beinvenue Batard Montrachet", which translated means "welcome Bastard" and turned possession over to him. Today, it is one of the most highly priced and prized vineyards of the Montrachet region.

રે

56

WINE SOAKED BRITISH TROOPS

John Talbot was killed in 1453 in St. Emilion when he and his troops were looking for some English troops in the area. Folklore has it that soldiers paused to sample the great wines of St. Emilion which turned into an all day drinking bout. Being somewhat drowsy from the wine, the soldiers lay down in the fields to snooze and the French garrison took advantage of their condition and ambushed the wine-soaked British troops. It is believed that Marshall Talbot was shot in the throat with an arrow.

ﻫ

DISCOURAGING LITTLE THIEVES

Chateau Duazac grand cru classe in Margaux is credited with discovering the cure for the mildew fungus that would attack the grapes, which would become useless as they withered. Nathaniel Johnston, then owner of Dauzac, some years past was annoyed by the practice of children picking his grapes on the vines that were close to the road. To discourage the little thieves, he sprayed the vines with a mild sulphur solution that turned the leaves an unappealing color. Then he discovered that the vines near the road that received this treatment were not affected by mildew. So experiments were carried out at other vineyards. Today the practice is still carried out by mixing copper sulphate, lime and water to control mildew.

ﻫ

"There is not a corner nor burrow in all my body where this wine doth not ferret out my thirst."

– Francis Rabelais (circa 1490) –

"If God forbade drinking, would he have made wine so good?"

– Cardinal Armand Richelieu 1585-1642 –

THE LEGENDS OF MUSCADET

Muscadet, a region near the mouth of the Loire River and famous for its crisp white wines, still maintains a local tradition that a bottle of wine must be drunk when a new vine is planted and three drops must be sprinkled on the stem and root. When a new road is built, the custom calls for the sprinkling of wine on each section that is completed. The Muscadet region has many legends and customs. Another is to make a hen hatch, then place her on eggs set in the nest by a drunkard. A popular tale that is still told in the Loire Valley is about the local drunk who removed all of his clothes to save his vines from a hailstorm. The children saw this act and told their parents and the story finally reached his wife. She became furious and was determined to cure her husband of his drunken habit once and for all.

When he fell asleep that evening, she placed a jug of water beside his bed and when he awakened in the morning, he sat up in bed, saw the water in his wine jug and died off shock. When they buried him, the town drunk, a vine began to grow on his grave. As the grapes ripened, they shed tears on his tombstone that attracted birds from around the whole region. The sight of this affected the whole town and most of them became drunk and began to act foolishly. So today, if someone is unkind to another, the ghost of the vintner stalks the streets and is said that his breath induces the mayor to act foolishly and the belief is he is looking for the water jug to tip it over. If someone spills a jug of water, it is immediately rinsed out with wine.

French grape growers are allowed to only own 100 acres of vines by law.

WIRE NETTNG ON SPANISH WINE BOTTLES

Marquis de Riscal is one of Spain's outstanding wines from the Rioja district. It has a wire netting covering the bottle with the ends of the wire sealed with a small lead seal. This netting is called Alambre in Spanish. The practice goes back many years to prevent pilferage of the famous label by less scrupulous wine producers who would like to sell their inferior wine under the Marquis de Riscal label which fetched a much higher price.

MARYLAND VS. FRANCE

Lord Baltimore once wrote in his report to King Charles I of England on the "state of the Colony" that 1622 was a good year for Maryland wine, that yielded considerable quantities of wine which were sold at a good profit...a vintage most pleasing to the palate, comparing favorably with the noblest Burgundies of France.

Wine proverbs at the Domecq winery in Mexico;

> "The owner drinks first from the pitcher,"
> "He who goes not with wine, goes with tears and signs."
> "One drop of wine my wine is worth more than all of your water."

–Said the Mosquito to the Frog –

"From vintaged vine and married women always shines a pleasant light."

"The pilgrim would be without his walking stick before he would be without wine."

"Wine and women cause the loss of one's senses."

THE SEVEN YEAR FOREST FIRE

Off the coast of Morocco is the island of Madeira, famous for its dessert wines. When the Portuguese landed on the island 500 years ago, they set fire to the woods that covered the mountainsides, and the forest fire burned for seven years. The wine makers feel that it is the ashes that enriched the soil and imparts that special quality in the wines.

Centuries ago, grapes were called "vegetable dragon pearls" in China.

PALM WINE

Historians believe that the first wine that man drank was made from palm trees. A slash was cut into the trunk of the palm tree to obtain the juice, which was then left to ferment in the warm Egyptian sun and was ready to drink the next day. Historians believe the time was about 4000 B.C.

THE VINEYARDS OF ENGLAND

Yes, Virginia, there are vineyards in England. Wine producing vines were transported to England during the reign of Emperor Claudius, in the year A.D. 43. The invasion of England was launched from the coast of France by a legion of 18,000 men commanded by Aulos Plautus. A soldier named Titus carried 55 wine shoots in earthen pottery. Although there were native vines in England previous to the invasion, they were not the winemaking varieties. After World War II, Winston Churchill promoted the growth of vineyards in England.

MOUTHWASH

New uses for wine emerged during the Renaissance (c. 1300-1600 A.D.). Guy de Cahuliac, a French army surgeon, recommended rinsing the mouth with wine to prevent dental decay. Dr. Johannas Dryander, a German, recommended that vermouth wine be used to minimize halitosis due to stomach upset.

MITHRIDATISM

King Mithridates of Pontus (c. 132-63 B.C.), always fearful that someone would assassinate him with poison, formulated a universal antidote of ingredients immersed (infusion, decoction) or dissolved in wine. The ingredients were small doses of poison which he concluded would counteract lethal doses. He was so successful that in 64 B.C. an attempt to commit suicide by taking poison failed and he had to have himself speared by a guard. In fact, he bequeathed us the work "mithradatism", which is the acquisition of immunity to poison by ingestion of gradually increased doses of it.

MIXING WINE AND WATER

In 1907, scientists at the Pasteur Institute in Paris confirmed that the addition of wine to water destroyed the causative bacteria of typhoid and cholera. As a result, Frenchmen in endemic areas were instructed to add white wine to water six hours before meals and red wine twelve hours prior to meals.

CHAMPAGNE AND INFLUENZA

In 1873, an English physician, Dr. Robert Druitt, became well known for advocating sherry wine as a cardio tonic, claret for gout and measles, and champagne for neuralgia and influenza.

❧

A POINT AND A HALF

The well-known aperitif wine "Punt E Mes" acquired its name from a stockbroker in Italy.

Years ago, people would order vermouth with bitters added by degrees of points. When a stockbroker was asked for his order of bitters to be added to his vermouth, he replied "Un Punt e Mes" (a point and a half). The name stuck and became world famous.

❧

THE PATRON SAINT OF THE BLIND

A Frenchman was experimenting with a wine drink flavored with quinine in the year 1830 and became blind. He prayed to St. Raphael, the patron saint of the blind, to restore his eyesight. When his prayers were answered, he honored the Saint by naming his new drink St. Raphael.

❧

CALIFORNIA'S FIRST VINES

One of the first commercial vineyards and wineries to be established in California was started by a Frenchman named Jean Louis Vignes in 1829 on the site where the present Los Angeles Union Station now stands.

The cost for the raw material (grapes before pressing) to make a bottle of Champagne in France is approximately $1.50 per bottle.

THE WINE THAT MAKES GRANDPA
FEEL TWENTY AGAIN

In the wine region of Tuscany, we find a little known wine called Vino Santo, which the Italians believe is supposed to engender warmth between husband and wife and make grandpa feel twenty again.

THE LOSS OF A HAND OR FOOT
FOR SMUGGLING WINE

In 1247, the exportation of Gattinara wine from the Piedmont district in Northern Italy was strictly controlled. Export was permitted only from the first of August to the first of October each year and during the feast of Santo Eusebio and All Saints. Anyone caught trying to smuggle wine out of the territory at any other time was condemned to the loss of not only the product but also his carts and ox teams and other vehicles in addition to a fine of 25 lire in Pavian coins. If the violator was unable to pay the sum, he had the choice of being deprived of either a hand or a foot.

❧

BEES AND ASTI SPUMANTE

Asti spumante originated as a spumante (foamy) in about 1870. Made from the muscat grape which is very ancient and has been identified with the grape called Apianae cited in numerous Latin scripts. The name is referred to the sweetness and aroma that attract bees (api).

❧

SPANNA AND THE SPANISH CHANCELLOR

The Nebbiolo grape was introduced into the Northern Piedmont provinces in the early fifteenth century by a citizen of Gattinara, a cardinal who had become chancellor to the king of Spain. He named the grape Spanna (the local dialect word for Spain) in his honor.

❧

THE BOAR AND DEER MENACE

In the Rheingau district of Germany, one of the big problems for growers is deer and wild black boar. When new vine plantings are planted to replace old uprooted vines the deer nibble the young tender leaves and the young vine dies while the black boar will uproot the whole plant.

To solve this problem, the growers take advantage of the many islands in the Rhine and plant the new vines there until they are sturdy enough to be replanted in the vineyards on the slopes which rise up to the forest. Some sections in the Rhine Valley where there are no islands and the deer and boar population is great, whole vineyards are abandoned.

૨એ

COME, SIT BY MY TOMB

The 14th century poet Hatez chose this inscription to be placed on his tomb, "Come and sit beside my tomb and bring wine and music. Feeling your presence, I shall come forth from my sepulcher, Oh, divine creature, let me contemplate you in all your beauty."

૨એ

CORKSCREW PENCILS

Bingen is a small wine village in the Hessia region of Germany which is across the Rhine River opposite Rudesheim and the local folklore is that the inhabitants carry corkscrews instead of pencils in their pockets and the corkscrews are humorously called Bingen pencils.

૨એ

PRECIOUS SOIL

Some of the small and famous vineyards in the Rhine Valley of Germany are so steep that retaining walls are built in terraces to hold the precious soil. When a heavy rainfall washes some of the soil down the steep hillside to the bottom, the vineyard workers will cart all the soil back up to the terraces in buckets and baskets on their backs to maintain the precious slate and soil necessary to produce a great wine.

❧

LONG NAME, SMALL LABEL

Eitelsbach (I-tells-bach), a small village on the Rower River in the Moselle region has a small vineyard owned by the Rautenstrauch family and the wine bears the full name Eitelsbach Rautenstrauch meaning "Carthusians Hill". The label is one of the smallest in Germany hence the local joke is "the wine with the longest name on the smallest label."

❧

THE BEAST OF LUXEMBOURG

In the tiny country of Luxembourg, the village Schwebsingen fountain spouts free wine. Legend holds that a path to the little hamlet was once dominated by a beast taller than trees and shaped like a horse who is only seen at night after one has visited the wine fountain.

❧

THE DRUNKARD'S LINE

A single track railway from Trier to Piesport which follows the winding Mosele is called the "Drunkard's Line."

⁊

"Give me wine to wash me clean of the weather-stains of cares."
– *Ralph Waldo Emerson – 1803-1882 –*

⁊

DRESSING WOUNDS WITH WINE

Galen, (c. 130-200 A.D.), perhaps the greatest physician after Hippocrates, also maintained that there was no better wound dressing than wine. While serving as a physician to the gladiators, he noted that wounds did not putrefy when the dressings were saturated with wine. In cases of evisceration, he bathed the viscera with wine before replacing them in the abdominal cavity.

⁊

Sherry devotees are fond of quoting these lines attributed to the patriarch of one of the great bodegas:

> I must have a drink at 11;
> It's a duty that must be done,
> If I don't have a drink at 11,
> Then I must have 11 at 1.

≈

"The wine cooper this day did divide the two butts of Sherry, which we did send for, and mine was put into a hogshead; it is the first great quantity of wine that I ever bought."

– Excerpt from Pepys' Diary
January 2, 1662 –

≈

Very Good in its way
Is the Uerzenay,
Or the silerry soft and creamy,
But Catawba wine
Has a taste more divine,
More Dulcet, delicious and dreamy . . .

– Longfellow –

≈

Early American Indians of the east coast called the native grapes Messamins, later identified as the Scuppernong.

≈

POTATOES, CABBAGE AND ORVIETO

Orvieto, one of Italy's popular white wines, is grown in the most unusual vineyard in the world. The vines share the ground with potatoes and cabbage that is planted throughout the vineyards with some of the vines climbing up through the branches of the trees and sometimes strung along overhead trellises.

A VILLAGE WINE FOUNTAIN

Each year on the first Sunday of October, following ancient tradition, the people of Rome and Latium gather around a fountain known as La Fontana die Mori, which for a day emits in place of water a perfumed white wine. The fountain is in the heart of Marino, one of the so-called Castelli Romani, little more than 20 kilometers from Rome on the Lake of Albano. That day, a festival of folklore and religion celebrates the victorious return of Marcantonio Colonna after winning the battle of Lepano on October 7, 1571, the epic encounter between Turks and Christians.

THE SPECIAL RAISIN
EATEN ON NEW YEAR'S DAY

In Tuscany, very ripe grapes are picked with great care so that intact bunches can be carried from the vineyards in shallow layers on trays so the grapes won't be crushed, and left to dry in the attic, where there is free air circulation from October to January. Sometimes, bunches are individually tied with string to the rafters (not in commercial operations). A plate of these special raisins is served by tradition at the end of every New Year's Day lunch, for if eaten on the first day of the year, it is believed they insure that you will not be short of money in the year to come.

In the sixteenth century, a Bishop who resided in the town of Trier in the Moselle Valley issued an official statement: "Whosoever, after drinking his ten or twelve bottles, retains his senses sufficiently to support his tottering neighbor...let him take his share quietly and be thankful for his talent...It is but seldom that our kind Creator extends to anyone the grace to be able to drink safely sixteen bottles of which privilege he hath held me, the meanest of his servants worthy." (Bottles were smaller in the sixteenth century.)

Wine is one of the most civilized things in the world, and one of the natural things that has been brought to greatest perfection. It offers a greater range for enjoyment and appreciation than possibly any other purely sensory thing that may be purchased.

– Ernest Hemingway –

THE OLDEST WINE ON EARTH

The oldest sample of wine known to exist in the world is in the German wine museum in Pfaz which houses many ancient winemaking tools from the days of the Roman occupation. An amphora dating back to the third century A.D. contains wine that is very cloudy which was determined by scientists to indeed wine.

ICE SAINTS

There are four days in Germany, May 12-15 which are called "Ice Saints" and it is this period of time when the greatest threat of frost exists and the names of these days are St. Pancartius, St. Boniface, St. Servatius and St. Sophia, often referred to as a Cold St. Sophia. Once the Saints' Days are over the growers feel a relief from the devastating threat.

FERTILIZING, NATURE'S WAY

Several Chateaux in the Haut Medoc still use horses to transport the grapes to the vat houses. Some say it is strictly tradition but others claim it is one way of fertilizing the vines, nature's way, and is beyond the strict rules on fertilization set up by "Appellation Controlee".

THE NAUTICAL CHATEAU

Chateau Beychevelle a fourth growth in St. Julien has an ancient sailing vessel depicted on its label with the sail lowered. This came about when Jean Louis de Nogaret received the title of admiral of France. He was the proud owner of the Chateau de Medoc and when he was in residence at the Chateau, all sailing ships had to lower their sails (baizzez les volles) as a salute to the admiral which became a nickname for the Chateau. Eventually, the name was changed to Bechevelle.

THE VINES THAT GAVE PRAISE TO GOD

Back in the early 1800s, many of the Great Chateau owners would instruct the vineyard workers to allow only two canes to grow from the large wine stock in the early spring and that the new canes were to be tied and trained with the tips pointing toward Heaven. This was a religious belief that if pointed skyward, they would praise God and he would reward the grower with a good crop. This belief persisted for many years until the scientific people did a little research to test the theory. It was established that this practice was very beneficial simply because of the fact that because the new canes pointing upward would retain the precious sap that was giving life to the vines whereas the other growers, who were not so religiously inclined would let the new canes grow horizontally along the vines with a lot of sap dripping out on the ground.

A PENNY FOR YOUR WINE

A winemaker's tip – when sampling a white wine and you suspect an excessive amount of hydrogen sulfide in the wine, drop a clean copper penny in the glass. (The copper will absorb the hydrogen sulfide.) Re-taste the wine.

73

THE CANNON OF CHATEAU CANTEMERLE

Chateau Cantemerle Grand Cru Classe` de Medoc is one of the first Chateaux one sees after Chateau LaLagune coming from Bordeaux as they enter the Chateau region of the Haut Medoc. If a visitor were to stop for a visit, he would probably hear the tale of how Chateau Cantemerle got its name and the story is that during one of the periods when the English and French were in one of their wars, British soldiers were camping on the estate. They stole and drank the wines stored at the Chateau and became very rowdy and began to harass the local residents until some of the French citizens remembered a cannon that was on the property and the canon was called the merle (blackbird). This cannon was loaded and fired with a startling roar which so scared the drunken British soldiers, they all fled. The chateau then became Cantemerle (the blackbird that sang).

ે**

"One glass of wine makes a woman lovely; with two glasses, she becomes hateful; at the third, she lusts invitingly; with the fifth, she will solicit any ass upon the streets."

– Greenblatt, R.B. (Search the Scriptures, J.B. Lippincott 186

ે**

"Drink no longer water, but use a little wine for thy stomach's sake and thine often infirmities."

– Timothy 12, 5:23 –

ે**

THE HONEYMOON AND HONEY WINE

Mead, a wine made from honey, was a favorite drink of the Gauls and Anglo-Saxons. The honey mead was a favorite wine served at all weddings. The ritual was that the bride was sent to bed early in the evening and the groom's friends would proceed to render him intoxicated with Mead. He would then be placed in bed next to his bride. As legend would have it, the power of the Mead honey wine would provide the sensual power for the groom to sire a son on his wedding night.

❧

HOW BURNT WINE BECAME BRANDY

One of the world's most famous wines is called Cognac and was discovered during the "thirty years war" in Europe between 1618 and 1648. Holland was a big buyer of wines from the Charente Region just north of Bordeaux called Cognac. The war had placed a heavy demand on the shipping trade which left very little deck space for the huge casks of wine. An enterprising Frenchman thought about the situation and concluded that wine contained about 80% water, so if the water could be removed, this would cut down on the bulk and that the same amount could be shipped in 80% less space with a huge savings on freight charges. Hence, the process of distillation (cooking the water out of the wine) leaving just the alcohol and the flavoring agent. When it arrived in Holland, all the Dutch would have to do was add water, and "voila" wine. The Dutch, being cautious business people, wanted to taste the cooked wine before they paid for the shipment. They were elated by the taste of the nectar and felt it would be a waste of good water to dilute this wonderful beverage and consumed it as is. The name they gave it was "Brandewign" which was Dutch for burnt wine, which was later Anglicized Brandy or Cognac from the region of France where it was made.

❧

THE LEAPING MOUSE

Meursault, a full-bodied white wine made primarily from the Chardonnay grape in and around the village of Meursault south of Volnay in the Cote du Beaune, is supposed to derive its name from the Latin Muris Saltus, which means leaping mouse. Legend has it that the Roman soldiers who were camped near the village would watch the mice jump across the local streams.

Montrachet, which means bald hill in French, has only 18 ½ acres, and is so prized for the wine it produces from the Chardonnay grape that it is not unusual to see French troops salute the vineyard when passing by.

IRRIGATING BY EVAPORATION

Theirry Manoncourt, owner of Chateau Figeac, a premier grand cru classe of St. Emilion, explains a unique method of inducing moisture back to the vines. The appellation controlee laws forbid irrigating the vineyards to prevent over-production and large yields to protect the quality of wine. However, many of the growers build shallow trenches at the ends of the rows of the vines to catch excess water from a rainfall. When they prune the vines, the clippings are placed in the water-filled trenches on the windward side. The clippings absorb the water and by evaporation the breeze blows the moisture back onto the thirsty vines. Just when the vine clippings become soggy and rotting it is time to prune again.

"Wine is a healthier beverage at meal time rather than milk for adults."

– Louis Pasteur –

THE MILLION DOLLAR WINE

Chateau Rayne Vigneau, A Premier cru classe wine from the Sauternes region of Bordeaux vineyards is situated over deposits of precious stones worth millions. Every time the workers cultivated the soil around the vines, they would discover a few of the precious stones when the earth turned. The owner of the chateau gave the workers permission to sell the gems and split the reward among themselves. The gem broker who was buying the stones became curious as to where these valuable stones were coming from. When the workers informed him that they were from the vineyards of Chateau Rayne Vigneau, the gem broker contacted a professional gemologist organization, which in turn received permission from the Chateau manager to conduct tests of the soil in the vineyard. They determined that over a million dollars worth of gems lay under the vineyard. When the owner was told of this exciting news, he was not in the least impressed for he placed more value on his vines and the wines they produced and forbade any excavation or mining of the precious gems. Chateau Rayne Vigneau is considered the million-dollar Sauterne because of the rich and valuable soil that it is planted in.

THOMAS JEFFERSON'S FAVORITE WINE

It is reported that Thomas Jefferson was responsible for Chateau Durfort Vivens rating as a second growth of the 1855 classification. When he was ambassador to France, he always praised the wines of Durfort Vivens as the best Margaux and, therefore, his praise greatly influenced the rating committee's judgment.

"In Bordeaux, there are as many people growing mushrooms as people growing wine."

"Wine drunken with moderation is the joy of the soul and the Heart", from the book of Aprochylin 180 B.C.

A STAND OFF IN BEAUJOLAIS

In the fourteenth century, the ruler of Beaujolais was surprised by a band of mercenary soldiers while he was out visiting his subjects in the country. They had seized the town of Anse and were looting and raising havoc. He immediately summoned his peasant army and proceeded to march on the town in rescue. But, he discovered that the mercenaries had barricaded themselves within the town walls. The ruler of Beaujolais was prepared to destroy the town and every mercenary with it. But he realized the cost in destroying plus the cost of rebuilding it. Estimating the cost, he offered the trapped mercenaries the same amount of money if they would promise to leave Anse and all of Beaujolais and never return. The mercenaries considered the offer – to be able to leave with their lives and receive money too – was too good of a deal to refuse, so they accepted and never returned to Beaujolais.

THE TALE OF CHAMBOLLE

Burgundy enjoyed fame for many years before people throughout Europe sought after Bordeaux and the wines. To keep their reputation, many of the vintners resorted to many strange superstitions and habits to insure their wines would not suffer some fateful disaster. One such superstition that is told regards a vintner in Chambolle who buries a toad under each vine to prevent hail and frost. They also believed that women are bad luck for the wines and the vineyards. French women to this day are not permitted in a wine cellar unless they are from another country and with an escort. Pregnant women are considered the worst threat and were absolutely forbidden in the vineyards. If it was discovered that one of the women working in the vineyards during the harvest was pregnant (usually the early months when she would not show) the whole vintage was expected to go bad.

THE ARCHITECT OF CHATEAU CLOS VOUGEOT

Chateau clos Vougeot in Burgundy, which is the seat and property of the Chevaliers du Tastevin promotional order, is the site of the monthly dinner of this organization. The dinner is held in the press house and members of this order are all dressed in colorful robes and meet in the interest of promoting Burgundy wines. The chateau was built back in the Middle Ages by monks of the Cistercian order and took over 200 years to complete. The monk who drew the original plans was so proud of his accomplishment that he signed the plans before receiving approval from his superior. His superior, or abbot, was so upset with the monk's self-pride that he ordered another monk to completely ruin the original design and built the castle with many flaws. It was such an awkward design that when it was completed, the monk died of shame on the spot.

Thomas Augustine Daly in his poem, "The First New Year's Eve":

> The man, the one and only one
> First Gentleman on earth
> Said: "How about a little fun?
> "Come, let us have some mirth!
> "To some swell nightclub we must roam,"
> Said he, "and drink champagne."
> But she said: "We can stay at home,
> "And still be raising Cain."

જ

A French belief is, "If there's a yarn worth spinning, then the wine is worth drinking."

જ

CHATEAU LAFITE THE WINE OF VIGOR

Chateau Lafite is credited with its early fame from an eighty-year-old gentleman, who after a full life of fast living, still had the stamina to take a young bride. When the King asked the Duc de Richelieu what he attributed his vigor and vitality to, he replied, "by drinking Chateau Lafite," which soon became the rage of Versailles.

જ

THE MINERAL WATERS OF CARBONNIEUX

Chateau Carbonnieux, situated in the Graves district of Bordeaux, once belonged to the church and the local fathers made fortunes by selling wines to Mohammedan Turkey which forbids alcohol. Charles Redding tells a story in a book he wrote a century ago, "To mystify Mahomet was a worthy and holy work for the children of the papist St. Bernet. So they exported their white wines, of which the limpidity was remarkable, as "the mineral waters of Carbonnieux". The French comment on the story is always the same: 'Better to sell wine as water than water as wine.'"

ꝰ

A MILLION VINEYARD DEEDS

Since the 1930s, more than a million vineyard deeds throughout France have been examined, but a scant ten thousand have been approved for classification.

ꝰ

"The patient should be given to eat what he wishes and wine to drink before the operation, so that he may not faint and may not feel the knife."

(Sanskrit Medical Book c. 2000 B.C.)

ꝰ

CHATEAU LAFITE NOW HAS PLUMBING

During the German occupation of France in World War II, high-ranking German Generals occupied many of the classic chateaux in the Haut Medoc Region of Bordeaux. The higher the rank of the general, the better the choice of the chateaux. The top ranked General took up residence at Chateau Lafite Rothschild. To his amazement, the chateau had no plumbing or electricity. So he set his staff to the task of installing the modern conveniences throughout the estate. When the job was finally completed, the war was over and Lafite was returned to its owner in a better state then when it was surrendered to the German's occupation. However, Chateau Cos d'Estournel, just up the road from Lafite, suffered considerable damage and it took a major restoration project to rebuild the chateau to its original state.

ॐ

CLARET OR GASCON

The red wines of Bordeaux for many years have been called Claret by the English and it is considered that Claret derives its name from the Earls of Clare, who under Henry II of England ruled Bordeaux during England's occupation. Before it was called Claret, it was called Gascon by the previous French owners.

ॐ

KNEEL TO DRINK

Dumas once said that Montrachet should be drunk kneeling with the head bared.

ॐ

'Tis better to drink and the next day feel bad than not to drink and wished you had.

છે

THE FRAUDULENT WINE

The Aimarques who were settled in the region of Nimes just North of Marseille, made a concoction called Vin de Sucre (wine of sugar). This artificial drink was manufactured without the use of grapes around 1903. The fraud was a mixture of sugar, water and tartaric acid. When the fermentation was completed, tannin and coloring agents were added. This practice was carried out until 1907, when the honest wine makers revolted with violent demonstrations, which forced the French government to pass a law prohibiting the "watering" of wines as well as a legal definition for wine.

છે

CHATEAU LAFITE FOR SALE

Classified ad in the London Gazette 1707: "To be sold: an entire parcel of new French Claret, being of the growth of Lafite, Margouze, and La Tour."

છે

WHITE LAFITE

Chateau Lafite Rothschild, the great classic Red Bordeaux wine made another wine that very few people had the pleasure of drinking and the rest of the world never heard about, "White" Chateau Lafite. A small section of Lafite's vineyard had white vines to make a white wine strictly for the Baron, his friends and family. The last white Lafite was made in 1959 and the vines were then uprooted. It is reported one of the last bottles of the '59 vintage was sold for $230.00.

IN VIEW OF THE RIVER

A favorite tale that persists among the growers in the Haut Medoc region is that if the vineyards can see the Gironde River, the wines will be first rate and the farther the vineyards are from view of the river, the lesser the quality.

CHATEAU HAUT BRION

Chateau Haut-Brion is an Irish name in origin, in ownership American, and birthplace France. Legend or myth has it that an Irish soldier settled in the Bordeaux region in the 13th century and started the vineyard. Pepsys, a famous writer in 1663 made mention of this wine when he visited "the Royal Oak Tavern in Lombard Street and here drank a sort of French wine called Ho Bryan that hath a good and most particular taste that I never met with."

THE STONE SAINT

Saint Vincent, the patron saint of wine, was admitted to Heaven after his death and was very sad and despondent and wandering around Heaven. God noticed his unhappiness and asked him why he was so unhappy. St. Vincent told the Lord it was because he had no time before his sudden death to say good-bye to his drinking friends and vintners of Burgundy. So, God gave him permission to go back to the vineyards to say good-bye to his friends. St. Vincent stayed longer than the time allowed. God sent a messenger to tell him to come back. When the messenger finally found St. Vincent, he was in the cellar of Chateau Mission Haut Brion drunk and full of good humor. When the messenger related the message that God had sent, St. Vincent refused to return. When God heard of this, he said "so be it" and changed St. Vincent into stone. He is still there in the "chai" of the Chateau Mission Haut Brion in a stone form of a bearded old drunken man clutching a cluster of grapes.

THE LEGEND OF CHATEAU RAUZAN GASSIES

There is a persistent tale often repeated to visitors in the parish of Margaux in the Haut Medoc region of Bordeaux about Chateau Rauzan Gassies 2nd Grand Cru Classe. This is one of the owners back in the early 1800s who had a liking for birds and always resisted advice to cut the tree line down at the rear of the estate to take advantage of the easterly prevailing winds that carried the moisture from the Atlantic Ocean. He, of course, insisted that the trees remain, so his beloved feathered friends would have a place to nest and raise their young. The tale goes on to tell that the birds were grateful for this consideration and when the vineyard was threatened with a devastating hail storm, the birds would perch on the vines and protect the precious berries with their wings.

MY HEART IS AT CALON

The label of Chateau Calon Segur , a grand cru in St. Estephe always has an outline of a heart on the label that encases the name of the Chateau. This dates back two centuries when the Marquis Alexandre de Segur owned the wine estates including Chateau Lafite and was reported to make the statement, "I make wine at Lafite, but my heart is at Calon."

❧

HISTAMINE, BLACK ROOSTER AND CHIANTI

The name chianti, according to legend, was derived from the Latin word "clangor" which referred to the sound from the hunters' trumpets that could be heard in the hills around the towns of Castellina, and Gaiole between Florence and Siena.

The black rooster used as the official seal on all grades of Chianti Classico is called the "Gallo Nero" black rooster. The black cockerel, the Etruscan symbol on the neck label of some Chianti Classico, bottles is dawn's bird chasing away the evil spirit of the night.

❧

Chianti Classico contains no Histamine. Histamine in wine causes headaches.

❧

THE STRAW BOTTLE

Legend has it that the straw found on Italian Chianti bottles was applied for a specific purpose other than as a decoration. Back in the days when refrigeration was scarce in Italy, straw was applied to act as a cooling factor. Workers would place the straw covered bottle in a cool stream to keep the wine cool and when the bottle was removed for consumption, the evaporating water from the soaked straw would continue to keep the wine cool.

❧

THE TEARS OF CHRIST

A once popular Italian sparkling wine is called Lacrima Christi and is extremely rare today. The name means "tears of Christ" and legend has it that when Christ returned to earth, he found this beautiful part of the world "inhabited by demons" and was so distressed that he cried and where his tears fell to the ground, up grew beautiful vines. A sparkling wine was made from its grapes which was on the sweet side and was so named "tears of Christ".

❧

BROLIO GROWLS

Brolio Chianti is world famous and is an estate in the Tuscan district of Italy. It is named after the ancient fortress in the medieval wars between Siena and Florence and a legend is often repeated that when Brolio growls, all of Siena would tremble. Dante was quoted as saying that some of the battles were so fierce that the small river Arbia flowed red.

❧

IT IS !

Est! Est! Est! is a white wine that is widely distributed in the United States. It has a slight sweet texture made from the Muscatello grapes near the village of Montefiascone just north of Rome in Italy. This wine owes its unusual name to a wine-loving German Bishop who was on his way to Rome. He would send his servant ahead to sample the wine in the different inns along the route and was instructed to write "Est" (it is) on the wall of every tavern that he found that served good wine. When the servant sampled the wines of an inn in Montefiascone, he was so excited about the quality of the wine that he wrote Est! Est! Est!. When the Bishop arrived, he stayed and drank himself to death. His tomb is in the village with this story inscribed upon it.

∂&

"Wine is the most hygienic and healthful of beverages."

– Louis Pasteur – 1822-1895 –

∂&

"Drink no longer water, but use a little wine for thy stomach's sake and thine often infirmities."

– Saint Paul (67 A.D.) –

∂&

"No wounds should be moistened with anything except wine, unless the wound is in the joint."

– Hippocrates 460-377 B.C.)

∂&

VERMOUTH

Vermouth evolved from the ancient days when the Romans added herbs, spices, gums and honey to disguise the taste of spoiled wines.

Vermouth became popular in the eighteenth century through the efforts of Antonio Carpano when he began selling a tonic wine in Turino Italy, made by steeping various herb extracts in sweetened brandy that has white wine added. Today, Turino is the center of the Italian vermouth industry.

An Italian who lived in Turin in the eighteenth century was trying to rid the local wine of its sweetness. He thought of something bitter. He added the flowers of Artemisia Absinthium to some wine and let it steep. The result was quite pleasing. Germans thought the combination was great and called it Wermut, their name for the herb we call wormwood. Thus vermouth was born.

❧

DRINKING FROM A COW'S HORN

The first wine beaker was probably a cow's horn. Egyptians and Persians before the time of Christ drank their wine from horns. The Greeks sipped wine from seashells.

❧

VERDICCHIO THE WINE OF COURAGE

Alaric, who was the leader of Visigoths, was marching on with his troops to conquer the city of Rome. To give his troops courage for the coming battle in the year 410, he carried over a thousand barrels of Verdicchio wine.

Madam de Pompadour used a wine-based cream to polish her own exciting royal complexion.

"Who after wine blathers about miserable things, about poverty, about the anguish of life."

– Poet Horace –

THE DEVILS VISIT TO WIESBADEN

One day the devil showed up at an inn in Wiesbaden in Germany to find out why so many people fell under his influence. The innkeeper, seeing the devil enter, said, "You look like the devil. The only thing that will save you is what we all here in Wiesbaden do to preserve us, to drink the wine of Wiesbaden that wells up from the ground. Five glasses a day is enough for any man or even ten. But you look so devilish and bad, you'll need fifty glasses a day for at least seven days. But if you do not complete the cure, you must leave and never return, for even the wine of Wiesbaden cannot help you." So the devil began to drink the fifty glasses a day on the first day and fifty on the second. At noon the third day, he asked for a rest, but the innkeeper held him to the cure. On the morning of the fourth day, the innkeeper handed the devil his first glass of the fifty, and the devil stared and started to scream and shudder and ran from the inn. Today the wine no longer wells from the ground and the devil has never been seen again, at least not in Wiesbaden.

HOW THE ALPS BECAME FROZEN

The source of the Rhine River in the Alps was once covered with green lush forms of vegetation and was owned by a farmer who placed the peak as a security for a shady loan. A mean magistrate confirmed the pledge when the farmer found it impossible to meet the demands of the loan. The neighbor who held the loan went up the green alp to inspect his new possession

. But when he reached the peak, thunder sounded and it began to rain. It so scared the new owner that he fell asleep and when he awakened at dawn, the alp was covered with ice and only a trickle was released by scant melting and produced the Rhine River which today is often referred to as a reminder to all men not to cheat their neighbors.

MONKEY ON THE BOTTLE

If you happen to see a bottle of German wine with a plastic gold colored monkey attached to the bottle in your favorite wine shop, it will be a red wine from near the Baden-Baden region made primarily from the Pinot Noir or Spatburgunder grape. This wine is produced from the region called Affenthaler and "Affe" in German means monkey. Therefore, its full name means wine from the "Monkey Valley". It is not one of Germany's best, in fact, it is rather mediocre to poor in quality.

THE SAINTS OF GERMAN WINES

Some unheard-of terms used in describing the many different types of German wines, which are illegal on a German label since the new wine law enacted in 1971 are:

St. Hubertuswein wines were harvested on November 3rd.

St. Martinswein means the grapes were picked on November 11th.

St. Katherinwein was gathered on the 25th of November.

St. Nikolauswein is picked on December 6th.

Christwein was vintaged on December 24th or 25th.

લ

Other German terms that are little used today and only locally are: Strumpfwein (stocking wine) is so bad and sour that it would mend a hole in a stocking.

લ

Fahnenwein (flag wine) is of such poor and offensive quality that, if one drop was to fall on the Regimental flag, it would shrivel and shrink.

લ

Preimannerwein is considered so strong that it would take three burly men to consume just one glass.

≈

Wenderwein is so sharp and acid that after drinking the wine, the imbiber is advised to turn over frequently during the night to prevent the acid from burning his stomach.

≈

THE DOCTOR OF BERNKASTLER

A Bishop in the fourteenth century who resided in the town of Trier of the Mosel is believed to have given Bernkastler Doktor its name, as he lay dying. On his sickbed, he declared that no medicine was of any help. A vintner from Bernkastler was paying his respects to the dying Bishop and left him a small cask of wine from his vineyards. The Bishop, after drinking several glasses of the wine, felt healthier and began singing praise for the vintner and called him the doctor of Bernkastler for his wine had done more to improve his health than all the medicine and physicians. That particular vineyard from which this wine came, is now known as the expensive Bernkastler Doktor.

≈

FASCHING IN GERMANY

Fasching is a very festive event in Germany that takes place when the wine from the last harvest begins to clear. This is usually just before Lent. Years ago, houses were decorated with large sheets of paper to disguise the shapes of the rooms with holes cut for doorways. Streamers were hung all over and elaborate scenes were painted on the paper. The new wines were drunk from Friday evening until Sunday night with people wearing the scantiest of costumes and most of the strict moral codes were relaxed. Today it is celebrated with more restraint but is still quite exciting.

"My manner of living is plain, and I do not mean to be put out of it. A glass of wine and a bit of mutton are always ready, and such as will be content to partake of that are always welcome. Those who expect more will be disappointed."

– George Washington –

THE BLACK CAT

Everyone who drinks wine is familiar with the German wine called Zeller Schwartz Katz meaning Black Cat. How this name evolved goes back to the time when people would go to a specific vineyard in Germany to buy their favorite wine direct from the producer. Of course, in those days the winemaker had no specific brand name. He was known strictly by his reputation. In the little town of Zell in the Mosele region, one winemaker always would keep the best wine in a separate vat toward the rear of his cellar and offered the rest for sale to the general public until someone noticed that the owner's pet cat which was totally black, always slept on top of a certain vat which was where the owner kept the best wine for himself. This particular wine buyer asked to buy some wine from the barrel where the black cat slept. It was then he discovered the better grade of wine. So he would tell his friends when they went to Zell to buy wines to seek out this particular wine from the cask with the black cat atop it. Hence, the title Zeller (town name) Schwartz (black) Katz (cat) originated.

FRITZ'S HELL

In the town of Neirsteiner in the Reinheissen region of the Rhine district, there is a vineyard called Fritzen Holle and the wine is bottled and sold under the name of Neirsteiner Fritzeu Holle. The vineyard where this wine comes from has a big hole on the slope of the vineyard and the owner's name was Fritz. Hole in German sounds the same as Hell and people would refer to this vineyard as Fritz's Hell.

❧

SUNDIAL VINEYARD

There is a little town nestled between Zeltinger and Bernkastler in the Moselle Region of Germany called Wehlen and is considered one of the best wine districts of the Moselle. The village faces an incredibly steep vineyard that has a massive section of slate protruding out on the slope which has a huge sundial painted on its face. Sonnenurh (Sundial) was the name adapted for this famous little vineyard in the town of Bernkastler, that usually commands the higher prices at the annual wine auction held in the town of Trier.

❧

MARRIED VINES

In many regions of the southern part of Italy, the vines are trained to grow on trees and this method is called Vite Alberato (married to) and the tree is called Marito (the husband).

EGYPTIAN WINES

The small amount of wine that is produced in Egypt is made in a region near Alexandria and most of it is consumed in Egypt. The wines are made from raisins rather than from fresh wine grapes, the quality is poor and the prices are high. However, to make up for the inferior and rather dull wines, some classic names have been devised, such as Clos de Cleopatre and Cru des Pyramides.

THE FATHER OF CALIFORNIA WINES

Agoston Haraszthy, the father of the California wine industry, was commissioned by the governor of California in 1861, who was enthusiastic about wines, to tour Europe and bring back cuttings from Europe. Haraszthy had planted a vineyard in the Sonoma Valley with the winery on a hillside with a lovely view and called it Buena Vista and was very successful, unlike the man from Bordeaux named Vignes who had planted many acres of imported vines from Europe in what is now Los Angeles. Haraszthy, however, had a touch for the vines. He chose the cooler climates of the north in Napa and Sonoma and Monterey, south of San Francisco. This is why the governor had chosen him to develop wine growing in California. After several months, Haraszthy returned with one hundred thousand cuttings from Germany, France, Jerez, Spain and Oporto, Portugal. All were labeled and tagged according to their type. The Civil War had come to California and no one was interested in wine making. Tags were lost, types and varieties were mixed and misplanted in the wrong regions. The Governor was very upset with Agoston refused to honor the contract with him. In disgust, Haraszthy went to Nicaragua to start a new venture and make his fortune in rum and coconuts. One day as he was crossing a stream, his horse reared and tossed him into the water, where he was eaten by alligators.

"Never think of leaving perfume or wines to your heir. Administer these yourself and let him have the money."

– Martial (40-102 A.D.) –

છ

"A house with great wine stored below lives in our imagination as a joyful house, fast and splendidly rooted in the soil."

– George Meredith –

છ

"There is a devil in every berry of the grape."

– A statement written in the Koran by Mohammed –

છ

CALIFORNIA WINES THRIVE DURING PROHIBITION

When the eighteenth amendment was enacted into law, Congress had left a loophole in the law that allowed the making of wine in the home. A group of growers banded together and formed the Fruit Industries Ltd. with a three million dollar loan from the very government that prohibited the making of alcoholic beverages. The new industry sold grape concentrates to the home wine maker. An additional service was also provided by a salesman who took the order. He would inoculate the grape concentrate once it was diluted with water with a pure wine yeast culture. He also supervised the fermentation, filtering, bottling and capping of the wine.

Other growers shipped their grapes in wooden boxes to large east coast cities with their large population of foreigners who had the know-how in making homemade wine. Business thrived all during the prohibition era.

THE WORLD'S LARGEST WINERY

Ernest and Julio Gallo started their wine-making business in a rented garage in 1933 with a grape crusher and a few redwood tanks purchased on credit. Today, they produce 45 million cases of wine a year and have storage capacity of a quarter billion gallons of wine. Gallo bottles one out of every four bottles of wine produced in the United States.

PART TWO

A SALUTE TO A VINEYARD

During the French Revolution, all the rulers of Europe were committing their armies to prevent the Revolution in France from spreading to other nations. Colonel Brisson with his French regiment was marching to join other forces of the Rhine and passed by Clos de Vougeot and its famous vineyards. He was overcome by a great pride for France and its famous wines and halted his troops and gave the command "left face" and ordered the regiment to dip its colors to one of France's great glories. Ever since, every French army unit that passes Clos de Vougeot has stopped and saluted the vineyards.

THE LORD IN VELVET PANTS

"Clos de Beze" which is just across a narrow road from the world-famous "Chambertin" is often referred to as the vine that is full, pungent of velvety bouquet with finesse and was described in P. Morton Shand's quotation of a Burgundian Vigneron, "One seems to have swallowed the Good Lord himself wearing velvet pants."

The Grand Duke Constantine of Russia (brother of the Czar) paid the staggering price of 20,000 gold francs for four barrels of Chateau Yguem of the 1847 vintage.

"To postpone the hour of death, drink Medoc at every meal."

– Author Unknown –

"After bread came wine, the creator's second gift for the sustenance of life, and first in order of excellence."

– Theatre of Agriculture, 1600 –

◈

THE SECOND OLDEST PROFESSION IN THE WORLD

The sommelier, a wine waiter, is considered the second oldest profession in the world, dating back as far as Ganymede, who served Ambrosia and Nectar to the gods on Mount Olympus.

◈

"I swear I will drink the first glass of wine neat, the second without water, and the third just as it comes out of the Barrel."

– (Oath taken by Honorary Vignerons of Bue.)

◈

Here rest Francois Gabriel
Charavin
Retired Captain – Member of
the Legion of Honor
Born in Bevrey,
February 9, 1785

He served his country
faithfully from 1809 to 1846
He made war in seven
kingdoms
Took part in twenty battles
One blockage and three
sieges

Under the reigns of Napoleon,
Louis XVIII
Charles X and Louis Philippe
He died on
December 16, 1870
Defending his vineyards

A Gallic Script on a Headstone in the French village Bevrey.

಄

FULL MOON AFFECTS THE QUALITY OF WINE

There still exists an ancient belief amongst some of the vintners in the Haut-Medoc region that harvesting the grapes during a phase of the full moon will affect the quality of the wine.

಄

"The flavor of wines is like delicate poetry."

– Louis Pasteur –

"In water one sees one's own face;
But in wine, one beholds the heart of another."

– French Proverb –

VAL POLESELA

Italy's Valpolicella is believed to evolve from ancient writings from as far back as the 1500s which referred to this area in Verona as "Val polesela". In 1543, Sarayna wrote, "The Valle Pulicella consists of many valleys and produces distinguished wines, black, sweet, robust and mature."

THE GOD SOMA

In ancient India, wine, because of its healing properties, was even worshipped as the god Soma. In fact, early Hindu physicians knew that wine eased pain, and used it as an analgesic.

A MEAL WITH ICE WATER

Don't make the mistake of ordering a good meal and then expect to enjoy it with ice water as a beverage. A rich meal without wine is like an expensive automobile equipped with hard rubber tires. The whole effect is lost for the lack of a suitable accompaniment. Rich and heavy foods which are unpalatable with water can only be appreciated with a suitable wine. Wine warms the stomach and hastens digestion.

– Roy Louis Alciatore, Prop. of Antoine's Restaurant, New Orleans –

ह

"Wine measurably drank, and in season, bringeth gladness to the heart, and cheerfulness to the mind."

– Ecclesiastics 31:28 –

ह

"Wine that maketh glad to the heart of man."

– Psalms 104:15 –

ह

"When you ask one friend to dine,
Give him your best wine!
When you ask two,
The second best will do."

– Henry Wadsworth Longfellow –

ह

THE STAR SPANGLED BANNER AND WINE

The Greek Anacreon, who wrote many poems praising the delights of wine, choked to death on a raisin which was taken as a warning for all wine lovers to take their grapes in liquid form. Anacreon is remembered in one of England's favorite drinking songs called "To Anacreon in Heaven". Given a different set of words, you would have Francis Scott Key's Star Spangled Banner.

❧

$28,000.00 FOR A BOTTLE OF WINE

A new record was established for the price paid for a single 24 oz. Bottle of wine on May 31, 1979 when Charles Mara, a package store owner in Syracuse, New York, paid $28,000.00 for the 1805 Chateau Lafite.

❧

"In the judgment of the house of Bishops the use of the unfermented juice of the grape, as the lawful and proper wine of the Holy Eucharist, is unwarranted by example of our Lord, and an unauthorized departure from the custom of the Catholic Church."

– A statement of the House of Bishops,
Protestant Episcopal Church,
Chicago, Oct. 26, 1886 –

❧

"When a woman wants to be beautiful, she seeks above all to be happy, because a rapturous heart makes the facial skin lovely. And to stay happy, and thus become most beautiful of face, it would not be bad to advise her to drink a little good wine that serves to brighten the spirits and color the face."

– Leonardo Fiorvanti
16th Century Surgeon –

৯৯

"Champagne speaks all languages."

– Unknown Prussian Diplomat –

৯৯

"Wine is the most healthful and hygienic of all beverages."

– Louis Pasteur –

৯৯

"There are two reasons for drinking wine: one is, when you are thirsty, to cure it; the other, when you are not thirsty, to prevent it … Prevention is always better than cure."

– Thomas Love Peacock –

৯৯

"Nothing more excellent or valuable than wine was ever granted by the gods to man."

– Plato –

❧

"Never did a great man hate good wine."

– Francois Rebelais –

❧

"A bottle of good wine, like a good act, shines ever in the retrospect."

– Robert Louis Stevenson –

❧

"Wines that heaven knows when
Had sucked the fire of some forgotten sun,
And kept it through a hundred years of gloom."

– Alfred Lord Tennyson –

❧

"Very good in its way is the Verzenay, or the Sillery soft and creamy, but Catawba wine has a taste more divine, more dulcet, delicious and dreamy."

– Henry Wadsworth Longfellow –

❧

The British statesman Canning is supposed to once have said, "Sir, the man who says he likes dry champagne, lies."

❧

Cutting through space with all my might
I cross horizons over the earth.
A dove not servile but of worth,
I cast across the world the scent
Of a new sherry vintage, meant
For drinking health and serenading mirth."

– The Andalusian poet, Barbadillo –

❧

"How often the cup has clothed the wings of
darkness with a mantle to shining light
From the wine came forth the sun. The orinet
Was the hand of the gracious cupbearer,
And my loved one's lips were the occident.
Between the white fingers the chalice of golden
Wine was a yellow narcissus asleep in a silver cup.

– From the Diwan of Principe Marwan (963 – 1009) –

❧

"Let Nepos serve you with sherry; you will think it wine of Satia. But he does not serve it to everyone – he drinks it only with a trio of friends.

– Martial (40-102 A.D.) –

108

Twenty-five centuries ago, in 539 B.C. Cyrus the Great had his troops carry wine on their march to Babylonia as a prophylactic measure against waterborne diseases.

"Wine, one sip of this will bathe the drooping spirits in delight beyond the bliss of dreams. Be wise and taste.

– John Milton –

THE SACK OF LIFE

"Sacke is the life, soul and spirit of a man, the fire which Prometheus stole, not from Jove's kitchen, but his wine-cellar, to increase the native heat and radical moisture, without which we are buy drousie dust or deal clay. This is nectar, the very Nepenthe the Gods were drunk with: 'tis this that gave Gannymede beauty, Hebe youth, to Jove his heaven and eternity. Doe you think Aristotle drank perry? Or Plata Cyder? Doe you think Alexander had ever conquered the world if he had bin sober? He knew the force and value of Sacke; that it was the best armour, the best encouragement, and that none could be a Commander that was not double drunk with wine and ambition.

–Thomas Randolph: Aristippus, the
Jovial Philosopher, 1630 –

THE TWELVE APOSTLES

A special Bodega in the town of Jerez, Spain is called "the Apostles". Built in the early 1800s, the cellar contains 13 large casks. The center and largest contains 33 butts (500 liters per butt) and is called "The Christ" with 33 butts to coincide to Christ's age when he was crucified. There are six small casks on each side – one for each of the twelve apostles.

છ

"Each glass of wine is a reaffirmation of the real culture of Europe."

– Author Unknown –

છ

BLOOD OF JUDAS

Sangue Di Guida is a local name for the hearty red wine produced in the Lombardy Region of Italy and the name means "Blood of Judas".

છ

The U.S. tax on a bottle of Champagne is $1.65.

છ

BLACK VELVET

A famous drink of the Victorian Days that consisted of mixing half champagne and half Stout beer was called Black Velvet. It was more popular than Brown Velvet, which consisted of half champagne, half port.

જ્જ

AN OVERHEARD CONVERSATION

Victor Borge, the famous pianist and comedian was visiting Mirassou vineyard in California and Bud Carroll of Mirassou was explaining that the wine must maintain a delicate balance between sugar and acid. Victor Borge replied after sipping the wine, "Yes, it does taste half-acid."

જ્જ

SCREWY WINE

Wine instructor: If a wine is not properly stored, the cork will dry out and it will have a corky taste.

Student: If a wine sealed with a cork may sometimes taste corky, will a wine sealed with a screw cap taste screwy?

જ્જ

"To our wine as it comes to birth mysterious
Voices breathe stories old and everlasting young."

– Inscription on a wine press in Alsace –

&

"Moselle, your river, the wine-bearing slopes
that flank you, Where Bacchus ripens the aromatic grapes."

– Poet Ausony 365 A.D. –

&

"Moselle, the soil is the father of the wine,
the vine, the mother of the wine,
and the climate is its destiny."

– Stefan Andres –

&

Written in an old Journal of Chateau d'yguem in 1787, "Sold this day to a Mr. Thomas Jefferson, one hoghead of our best wine. We all cried a little."

&

"Bring me a flagon, enough for a dragon,
and fill it with chateau Y'guem."

– A. P. Herbert –

છે.

"Just why, I can hardly explain, but when for wine in Paris I call,
That bad wine comes in a big glass, and the Good wine comes
in a small.

– Unknown –

છે.

"You can't be gay without drinking Voulnay."

– Poet Ausonious –

છે.

NO PHYLLOXERA IN CHILE

Chile is the only wine growing nation that has never been affected by the dreaded phylloxera louse. The high Andes and strong Pacific breezes guard against Argentine infection, the northern desert of Atacama bars the way from Peru.

"Wine the cheerer of the heart
And lively refresher of the countenance."

– Thomas Middleton & William Rowlet –

ਟੈ

And Noah he often said to his wife when he sat down to dine, "I don't care where the water goes if it doesn't get into the wine."

– Gilbert Keith Chesterton –

ਟੈ

"Wine is the intellectual part of a meal,
Meats are merely the material part."

–Alexandre Dumas –

ਟੈ

"If food is the body of good living, Wine is its soul"

– Clifton Fadiman –

ਟੈ

"Wine is a constant proof that God loves us and loves to see us happy."

–Benjamin Franklin –

ਟੈ

"The slowly unfolding story of wine and food contains the saga of human culture, good manners and well being."

– Crosby Gaige –

❧

"Wine gives strength to weary men."

– Homer, 850 B.C. –

❧

"Wine in medicine is most beneficial; dark wine is most favorable to bodily growth, white wine is thinnest and most diuretic; yellow wine is dry and better adapted to digesting food."

– Greek physician Minesitheus –

❧

In Ernest Hemingway's novel, "Across the River and into the Trees," he refers to Valpolicella as "Light, dry, red and warmhearted like the house of a brother one gets along well with."

PART THREE

THE LANGUAGE OF WINE GLOSSARIES

THE LANGUAGE OF WINE

Wine has its own universal language, and to understand the fundamentals of wine, it is easier if you know its vocabulary. The following is an elementary glossary of the basic, more commonly used terms that will help you to better express yourself when you 'talk' wine.

Acidity	The essential natural sourness which gives a bite on the tongue. It is an important keeping quality and contributes to bouquet.
Aftertaste	The sensation (good or bad) after the wine has been swallowed.
Astringency	The quality causing a mouth to "pucker". This is due to the amount of tannin the wine has absorbed from the skins and seeds of the grapes, and will lessen with age.
Balance	The best combination of physical components (alcohol, fruit, acid) and the less tangible grace elements of "breed", "character", and "finesse".
Body	The consistency, thick and/or thin (big or light) of a wine, with an accompanying meaty or easy swallow.
Character	A complexity that shows distinctive and unmistakable qualities (color, bouquet, taste) of a particular type of wine.
Clean	The neutral and refreshing feeling on the tongue after swallowing wine.
Delicate	The light and agreeable flavor.
Dry	The complete absence of sweetness, due to complete fermentation.
Earthy	A mineral or organic taste of the soil or terrain.
Fine	Superior overall quality and complexity.
Flat	Dull and uninteresting, usually from low quality and acidity.
Full	Pleasantly strong in flavor, taste or bouquet.
Hard	Extreme dryness and above-average acidity (opposite of mellow or soft).
Heady	A wine of generous alcoholic content.
Light	A wine of generous alcoholic content.
Mellow	Soft and smooth, and of low astringency.
Nutty	A crisp and almost salty taste (as in Sherry).
Rich	A full combination of fruit, flavor and body.
Ripe	A wine in its full bloom of maturity and mellowness.
Robust	A hearty, full-bodied and strong flavored wine.

Soft   A mellow and smooth wine of low astringency.

Sour   A disagreeably sharp, acidic taste.

Sweetness The presence of sugar in a wine.

Tartness   Possessing agreeable fruit acids giving a sharp taste.

A WINE VOCABULARY (IN FRENCH)
FOR WINE LOVERS

French	English
Vin (van)	Wine
Chateau (sha-tow)	Estate
Mise (or Mis) en bouteille au chateau (mees on boot-taye o – sha-tow)	Bottled at the property where it is made
Nergociant (ner-gow-see-awn)	Wine Merchant, Shipper
Annee (ann-nay)	Year
Millesisme (mieel-es-eem)	Vintage
Chai (shay)	Cellar
Maitre de Chai (maytre deh shay)	Cellar Master
Cru Class (crew classay)	Classified Growth 1855 Bordeaux Classification
Vigne (veegne)	Vine
Vignoble (veegnoble)	Vineyard
Raisin (ray-sun)	Grape
Vendages (vawn-dawnges)	Harvest
Appellation Controlee (a-pell-ah-syon kon-trow-lay)	French Seal of Approval for the Consumer
Frais (fray)	Fresh
Sec (sek)	Dry
Doux (doo)	Sweet
Liquoreux (lik-or-rer)	Very sweet

Vieux (vee-yer)	Old
Juene (juh-ne)	Young
Bon (bonn)	Good
Mauvais (mo-vay)	Bad
Petit (peh-tee)	Small

GERMAN WINES

Americans are drinking more German wines today than ever before. Every 7th bottle of imported wine consumed in the United States comes from Germany. 85% of the wines produced in Germany are white wines and they outsell French white wines in the American market. Germany is the 8th largest wine producer in the world, with American demand up over 110% in the last eight (8) years.

Under the new laws for the production of all German wines, three categories have been established.

Tafelwein (Taf-fel-vine) — Table wine, light pleasant blended wines consumed mostly in Germany, can not use a vineyard name.

QBA (Qualitätswein Bestimmter Anbaugebiete) Quality wines which are checked by government laboratories (can have added sugar). Must come from certain regions (11) and grape varieties, can use vineyard name. Each bottle carries government approval number (A.P.)

Qualitätswein Mit Praedikat (kval-ee-tates-vine Mit Pray-dee-kat) Top category, may not be sugared. These are finest estate wines, with special attributes, as follows:

Kabinett (Kab-ee-net) — Lightest and driest of Praedikat category.

Spatiese (Shpate-lay-zeh) — Late picked grapes that are left on the vine and picked later than the regular harvest.

Auslese (Ow-slay-zeh) — More body and sweeter wine from specially selected extra ripe clusters of grapes.

Beerenausiese (Beer-en-ow-slay-zuh) Individually selected berries, luscious and sweet.

Trockenbeerenauslese (Trock-en bearen-ouse-lay-zeh) Produced from over-ripe grapes left on the vine until they are almost raisins. Very sweet, used mostly as a dessert wine.

Eiswein (Ice-vine) — Made from grapes, harvested and crushed while still frozen.

There are 11 designated regions for quality wine. Most important are:

Nahe

South of the Rhine, fresh and racy, from Riesling grape, dividing line between Rhine and Moselle regions. Best Villages: Kreuznach, Schloss-Bockelheim.

Rheingau

One of the most famous viticulture districts of world, 80% are from Riesling grapes. Best Villages: Hockheim, Eltville, Raunenthal, Erback, Hattenheim (Steinberg), Winkel (Schloss Vollrad), Johannisberg (Schloss Johannisberg).

Rheinhessen

Mostly Silvaner grape, second largest wine region, home of Liebfraumilch (Milk of the blessed Mother), Best Villages: Oppenheim, Nierstein, Bingen.

Rheinpflaz or Palatinate

Largest wine region, Muller-Thurgau grapes, mellow wines with more body due to warmer climate. Good for everyday consumption. Best Villages: Forst, Deidesheim, Durkheim, Wachenheim.

Mosel-Saar-Ruwer

Saar and Ruwer are tributaries of Mosel-Steep wine terraces, Riesling grape. Mosel wines come in green bottles, Rhine wines in brown. Best Villages: Wiltingen, Ockfen, Ayl (Saar), Maximin Grunhaus (Ruwer), Piesport, Branueberg, Bernkastel, Graach, Wehlen, Zeltingen, Erden, Uerzig.

Franken

Along river Main, Silvaner grape produces earthy, robust, dry wines sold in flagon shaped bottles (Bocksbeutels). Best Village: Wurzburg.

❧

GLOSSARY

Abfullung (Ahb-fool-ung)   Bottling or bottler, must be listed on all quality wines.

Bereich (Buh-ryke)   District within a gebiet (region).

Croever Nacktarsch   (Crow-ver-Nak-tarsch) "Naked Bottom".

Dom   Cathedral.

Edelfaule (Aid-ee-foy-luh)   Noble not responsible for Trockenbeeren-auslese.

Erzeuger Abfullung (Air-tsoy-ger-Ahb-fool-ung) Estate bottled by a producer, not a shipper.

Furst (Fuhrst)   Prince.

Graf (Grahf)   Count.

Grosslage (Gross-log-uh)   "Collec-tive site," composite vineyard, made up of number of individual vineyards (Einzellagen) within sub-region or Bereich.

Keller   Cellar.

May Wine   Rhine wine with woodruff herbs infused.

Moselbleumchen (Mozl-blum-shun) "Little Moselle Flower," Moselle answer to Liebfraumilch.

Oechsle (Erks-luh)   Scale for measuring sugar content of grape wine.

Riesling (Reese-ling)   One of the great white wine grapes, used for best wines of Rhine and Mosel.

Roseewein   Rose wine.

Rotwein (Raht-vine)   Red Wine.

Schaumwein (Sh-own-vine)   Sparkling Wine.

Schloss   Castle.

Sekt (Zect)   Sparkling wine.

Spritzig   White wine with slight effervescence.

Staatsweingut (Shtots-vine-goot)   State wine estate.

Trocken   Dry.

Weingut (Vine-gut)   Domaine or vineyard property.

Weinkellerel (Vine-keller-eye) – Cellar.

Weinstrasse   Wine rood.

Weisswein (Vise-wein)   White wine.

Winzergenossenschaft (Vin-ser-gen-ohs-en-schahft) Co-op of wine growers.

Winzerverin (Vin-ser-vere-eyn)   Producers co-op.

Zeller Schwarze Katz (Tsel-ler-Swartz-Kats) "Black Cat of Zell."

WINE PRONOUNCING GLOSSARY
AND DICTIONARY

Aloxe-Corton (ahlox cor-tawn)   Northernmost village in Burgundy's Cote de Beaune.

Aligotè (ah-lee-got-ay)   Lesser white grape of Burgundy.

Amontillado (ah-mon-tee-yah-doe) A particular style of medium-dry Sherry.

Aszú (ahs-zoo).   Sweet grade of Hungarian Tokay.

Bacchus (bah-kuss).   Roman God of wine.

Beaune (bone)   Central village of the Côte de Beaune, home of Burgundy wine trade.

Bodega (bo-day-gah)   Spanish wine cellars, usually above ground.

Botrytis Cinerea (buh-trytis sin-area) Noble rot-Pourriture noble (see), called Edelfäule in German.

Bourgogne (boor-go-nyuh)   French for Burgundy.

Bual, or Boal (boo-ahl)   Grape used to make sweet Madeira

Cabernet Sauvignon (ca-bear-nay-saw-vee-n'yon). Classic red wine grape of Bordeaux and California.

Carafe   Glass bottle or decanter used in restaurants for "house wines".

Catawba (ca-taw-ba)   American wine grape producing sweet wines with grapey taste; backbone of most Eastern American sparkling wines.

Cave (cahv)   Wine cellar located underground.

Chai (shay)   Ground-level warehouse in Bordeaux. Opposite of Cave.

Chaptalization (shap-tally-zah-see-yon) The addition of sugar to the fermenting wine must – to build up the alcoholic content.

Chardonnay (shar-duh-ny)   The wine grape of French white Burgundy, Champagne and America's finest white varietal.

Chasselas (shass-lah)	White wine grape; in Switzerland, called Fendant.
Chãteau (shah-toe).	Synonymous with vineyard in Bordeaux.
Chenin Blanc (shay-nan-blahn)	White wine grape from the Loire Valley and California.
Clos (clo)	French for walled vineyard.
Cold Duck	Half sparkling Burgundy, half Champagne, producing slightly sweet, fruity drink.
Commune (caum-yoon)	French for a town or village.
Concord	American grape used for grape juice, jellies and sweet unsubtle wine.
Corbières (cor-b'yair)	V.D.Q.S. wine region of Southern France.
Côte de Bourg (kote deh boorg)	Dry red wine area, across Gironde from Medoc.
Cru (crew)	Literally, growth, but synonymous with vineyard.
Cru Classe (crew clah-say)	Classified browth, or vineyard of Bordeaux.
Cuvee (coo-vay)	A blend of wines.
Dão (down)	Light red and white table wines from Portugal.
Delaware	One of the best of American white wine varieties, often used in eastern American sparkling wines.
Dionysus	Ancient Greek God of wine.
Domaine (doe-main)	French for wine estate.
Douro (doo-roe)	River in north Portugal that flows through the Port district.
Egri Bikavér (egg-ree bee-ka-vair)	Full-bodied red wine from Hungary.
Enology (ee-noll-e-gee	Study of wine and winemaking. Also spelled Oenology.
Entre-Deux-Mers (ahn tr-duh-mair)	White wine district in Bordeaux.
Fermentation	The breakdown of sugar, by the action of the enzyme in yeast, into ethyl alcohol and carbon dioxide. Turns grape juice into wine.

Filtering	Clarification of wine by passing it through a material that removes suspended particles.
Fining	Clarification of wine by passing a material through it that coagulates suspended particles and precipitates them out.
Finger Lakes	Most important American wine district outside California.
Fino (fee-no)	A particular style of dry Sherry.
Fixin (feex-an).	Northernmost commune of Côte d'Or.
Flor	"Flower," white yeastly film that forms on top of some casks of Spanish sherry; they become Fino sherries.
Fumé Blanc	White wine made in California, from Sauvignon Blanc grape.
Gamay (gam-may)	Grape used in California and France for Beaujolais style wines.
Generic (jen-eric)	Wine names such as Burgundy, Chablis and Sauterne named after a wine region that has ceased to have any significance of geographical origin.
Gigondas (she-gown-das)	Full-bodied red and rose wines from Rhone village of same name.
Gironde (she-rownd)	Area in southwest France containing Bordeaux region.
Green Hungarian.	Light wine from California, not colored green.
Grenache (greh-nahsh)	Grape used to make red and rose wines.
Grey Riesling	California name for grape called Chaucé Gris, in France.

Gumpoldskirchen (goom-poles-kir-ken) One of the best white wines of Austria.

Hammondsport	Central wine valley of New York Finger Lakes district.
Haro (ha-ro)	Center of Rioja wine trade.

Haraszthy, Agoston	Hungarian emigré – "the father of California viticulture."
Haut (oh)	Literally, high; not necessarily an indication of higher quality.
Hectare (hecktar)	Mertic measure of area (2.47 U.S. acres).
Hectoliter (heck-toe-liter)	Metric measure of volume (100 liters or 26.42 U.S. gallons).
Hospices de Beaune (oh-speece duh bone)	Charitable hospital in Burgundy that owns many fine vineyards and auctions them to raise money.
Hudson River Valley	Oldest wine-growing district in U.S. (one hour from New York City).
Hybrid	A genetic cross between two different varieties or species of grapes.
Jerez (hair-reth)	City in southern Spain, center of Sherry production.
Kir	Popular aperitif made by mixing dry white wine with Cassis Liqueur.
Lees	The dregs or sediment left at the bottom of a cask after the wine is racked.
Liter	Metric liquid measurement equaling 1.06 quarts.
Lambrusca	The species of grapes native to North America.
Madeira	Sweet or dry wines, always fortified. (See Bual-Malm-sey-Rainwater-Sercial.)
Maderization	Brown tinge which poorly stored or old white wine acquires.
Malbec (mal-beck)	Red wine grape used to soften Cabernet Sauvignon in France.
Malmsey (mahlm-zee)	Richest and sweetest kind of Madeira.
Manzanillia (man-zah-nee-yah)	Very dry style of Sherry.
Mendocino	Northernmost wine area in California.

Merlot (mare-lo)	Grape used in Medoc (especially in St. Emilion and Pomerol), Italy, and California.
Midi (mee-dee)	Aera in southern France thats upplies much ordinary wine.
Mise en bouteilles (meez ahn boo-tay)	Bottled (his phrase on a wine label is followed by the name of a producer or wine shipper).
Monopole (mo-no-poll)	Specially selected wine backed up by the name of the shipper.
Monterey	City in central California. One of the most promising wine regions.
Montilla (mon-tee-ya)	Village in Spain near Jerez, producing light, unfortified wines used as aperitifs.
Mousseux (moo-suh)	French sparkling wine from outside Champagne area.
Must	Grape juice to be made into wine.
Napa	Village and county in northern California producing some of the best wine in the United States.
Niagara	Popular Eastern United States grape.
Neuchâtel (nuh-shah-tell)	Swiss white wine product from Chasselas grape.
Oloroso (oh-lo-ro-so)	A particular style of Sherry, used as a base for Cream Sherry.
Oxidation	Changes in wine due to air contacting the wine. (See Maderiza-tion.)
Oporto	City in northern Portugal, center of Port wine trade.
Pasteurization	Heating wines to sterilize them so any organisms present are destroyed.
Pétillant (pet-tee-yahn)	Lightly sparkling.
Petit (puh-tee)	Small
Phylloxera (fil-lox-uh-rah)	Insect that destroyed most of the world's vineyards in the 19th century.

Pinot Chardonnay (pee-noe shar-doe-nay) Classic white wine grape of Burgundy and California.

Pinot Noir (pee-nee nwahr) Classic red wine grape of Burgundy and California.

Pommard (poh-mar) Village in Burgundy's Côte de Beaune.

Pourriture Noble (poo-ree-toor nohbl) Noble rot; responsible for the unique flavor of Sauternes and Barsac. (See Botrytis.)

Premier Cru (preh-m'yay crew) First growth; refers specifically to some of the best individual vineyards in Bordeaux and Burgundy.

Puttonyos (pu-tohn-yos) Literally, baskets; used as a measurement to indicate the comparative sweetness of Hungarian Tokay (5 puttonyos is the sweetest). (See Aszú & Tokay.)

Racking Removal of clear wine from deposit on bottom of the tank by siphoning or pumping.

Rainwater Light-dry Madeira.

Retsina (ret-see-nah) Greek wine flavored with resin.

Rioja (ree-ohn-ha) Finest wine district of Spain.

Saké (sah-keh) Colorless Japanese beer, made from rice, served warm and sipped from porcelain cups.

Sangria (san-gree-eh) Spanish red wine with fresh fruits and soda water added.

Sauvignon Blanc (saw-vee-n'yohn-blahn) Used with Semillon for white Graves and Sauternes.

Scuppernong Native American grape; grown in the South for full-bodied sweet wines.

Sec (French), Secco (Italian) (sek, say-co) Dry.

Sediment The lees or deposits thrown off by a wine as it ages. Racking (see) will reduce it, a part of normal aging.

Sèmillon (she-mee-yohn) Fine white wine grape of Bordeaux and California.

Sercial (sair-see-al) Palest and driest of Madeiras.

Solera (so-lair-ah) Blending system used to make Sherry.

Sommelier (so-mel-yay)	Wine steward.
Sonoma	One of California's finest wine districts. A county and city just north of San Francisco.
Sulphurization	Slows down fermentation and aids in producing a sound wine. Excess leads to unpleasant smell and taste of sulphur.
Tannin	Drawn from grape skins and stems. Causes "puckeriness" when in excess. Gives character and long-lasting quality.
Tastevin (taht-van)	Shallow silver tasting cup used in Burgundy.
Tokay (toe-kie)	Sweet wine of Hungary. See Aszù.)
Toneau (tawn-oh)	Standard wine measure in Bordeaux. One toneau yields 96 cases.
Ullage (oo-lahj)	French term for air space in a bottle of wine, caused by slow evaporation.
Valdepeñas (val-day-pain-yass)	Wine village in central Spain.
Varietal	Term used in United States for wines labeled by grape variety from which they are made. Opposite of generic (see).
V.D.Q.S.	Step below Appellation Controlée – Vins Délimités de Qualité Superieur.
Vinho Verde (veen-yoh vair-day)	Literally, green wine; young red and white wines from northern Portugal.
Vinifera (vin-if-uh-rah)	Grape species responsible for most of the world's wines.
Vino Rosso	Red wines in Italian – in California refers to a mellow red table wine.
Wine Institute	California industry's association of wine producers.
Zinfandel (tzin-fan-dell)	Red wine grape grown extensively in California.

ISBN 141201889-7

9 781412 018890